W9-CKS-943

"You have heard it said, 'Faith without action is useless,' and I say to you, 'J. Philip Wogaman has anything *but* a useless faith.' His action—surrendering his sixty-year-long ordination with the UMC—was the logical, responsible, and loving manifestation of his commitment to fulfilling the role of United Methodist minister with integrity. *Surrendering My Ordination* reminded me not only of how far the church has yet to travel in its full inclusion of LGBTQ individuals but also of why I still have hope for such a transformation. I'm grateful for the honest and unashamed choice by Wogaman to demonstrate his conviction that the love and care for human beings (especially those on the margins) is more important than anything else, come what may. May his strength of conviction inspire you, as it did me, to live love regardless the cost."

—Colby Martin, Teaching Pastor, Sojourn Grace Collective, and author of *Unclobber: Rethinking Our Misuse of the Bible on Homosexuality*

"Why would someone who loves ministry give up his ordination credentials voluntarily? Why would someone who deeply loves The United Methodist Church critique it? In *Surrendering My Ordination*, Phil Wogaman tells the story of what led him to stand before his clergy colleagues and give up his ordination credentials, returning him to lay status in the church. Wogaman powerfully grounds his actions with a theological, ethical, and pastoral examination regarding the nature of ordination. As the special session of the General Conference approaches, Wogaman invites the reader into a conversation to consider ways forward for the denomination regarding the inclusion of gay and lesbian people in the life and ministry of the church. This thoughtful book ought to be read by lay and clergy alike."

—Bishop Karen Oliveto, The United Methodist Church, and author of *Together at the Table: Diversity without Division in The United Methodist Church*

"*Surrendering My Ordination* poignantly portrays the process by which a devoted pastor and respected Christian ethicist reached the decision to surrender his ordination as an act of protest and solidarity. In sharing his story with humility nurtured in grace, Dr. Wogaman provides insight into a life devoted to justice and inclusion. Though he cautions against others surrendering their orders, he bears witness to a process by which we can move beyond mere words to actions on behalf of the excluded."

—Bishop Kenneth Carder, The United Methodist Church, and Ruth W. and A. Morris Williams Professor Emeritus of the Practice of Christian Ministry, Duke Divinity School

"One of the great unsolved mysteries for church historians to ponder is why The United Methodist Church compromised the witness of Jesus, the inclusive love embedded in the Bible, and the long justice history of Methodism by approving language and legislation that proclaims 'The practice of homosexuality is incompatible with Christian teaching.'

Dr. J. Philip Wogaman represented many of us when he turned in his clergy credentials as a response/protest to that language and legislation when it was used to deny the journey to ordained ministry of a person who possessed all the attributes for effective ministry. Dr. Wogaman's book about his journey in ministry that led to a voluntary relinquishing of his ordination credentials is a must-read for those in The United Methodist Church and beyond who link their biases to the Bible. Many of us couldn't believe that a denomination that acknowledged its history of misusing the Bible to justify slavery, segregation, and prohibitions against the ordination of women would approve language and legislation in 1972 that resulted in the charging trials and suspension of same-gender-loving clergy candidates and clergy who performed their marriages.

This book will challenge those who engage in the 'violence of silence' as they have allowed and continue to allow the UMC to tarnish its justice history by discriminating against same-gender-loving clergy and the clergy who support them. And it will hold up a mirror before those who claim to be 'Christian traditionalist evangelicals.' We have seen the damage they have done to the UMC since 1972. And now we are living amid the damage they are doing to the United States and the world.

Martin Luther King said 'Injustice anywhere is a threat to justice everywhere.' Phil Wogaman shares his personal journey and in so doing reveals his journey to be one of steadfast loneliness, even among some so-called United Methodist 'progressives.'

Phil, I believe that if he were alive, Martin Luther King Jr., our Boston University School of Theology classmate, would endorse your book. You have 'walked your talk' as did MLK; may your story encourage more of us to do that."

—Gilbert H. Caldwell, cofounder of Black Methodists for Church Renewal and coproducer of the documentary film *From Selma to Stonewall: Are We There Yet?*"

"For twenty-five years, I have admired Dr. Wogaman for his compassion, his kindness, and his deep intelligence. Being an ordained minister seemed an obvious calling for him, and it never occurred to me while he was my minister when I was growing up that he would ever not be a minister. Now, after reading *Surrendering My Ordination,* I admire him more than ever and see his continued ministry through this beautifully written book. As a Christian and a Methodist, I am grateful for Dr. Wogaman's detailing his views on the meaning of ordination. As a person, I am grateful for his generous honesty in sharing his own spiritual journey over decades to seeing people for their actions and their faith, not for their gender or whom they love. I also appreciate Dr. Wogaman's candor around what he doesn't understand and doesn't know. For someone who clearly believes it is the Christian imperative to honor and sanctify committed love between two people, it now would never occur to me that such a principled man could do anything other than surrender his ordination at this moment in The United Methodist Church."

—Chelsea Clinton

"I was at the Baltimore-Washington Annual Conference when Dr. Wogaman surrendered his credentials to Bishop LaTrelle Easterling. I had been on the job as the Executive Director of Reconciling Ministries Network for one day, and his action both brought tears to my eyes as I saw yet another way the church's discrimination harms people and ushered me into the middle of the movement for justice in The United Methodist Church. As I read this book, I got that *Wow!* feeling I had that first day all over again as I truly came to understand not only the personal meaning that his ordination held for him but also the deep commitment that led him to surrender something held dear for so long because the church is doing harm to itself and to LGBTQ people by not acknowledging the gifts of those called to ordained ministry. 'Sin is any attitudes, acts, or practices that stand in the way of receiving the grace of God': Dr. Wogaman's words in one of the early chapters stayed in my mind as I read his book. Those same words also follow me as a leader in a church that is 'getting it wrong' as we continue the quest for justice that Dr. Wogaman models for so many."

—Jan Lawrence, Executive Director, Reconciling Ministries Network

"Following a lifetime of Christian service as a noted seminary professor, pastor, and church leader, J. Philip Wogaman provides an impassioned and deeply thoughtful explanation of his 2017 decision to set aside his United Methodist ministerial credentials in response to his church's exclusion of LGBT Christians from ordained ministry.

In contrast to so much of contemporary protest culture, Wogaman's testimony is distinguished by his continuing deep love for the church whose policies he calls into question and by the humble, reasoned, and wide-ranging theological account he gives of his own action. This is constructive criticism in the best sense, offering pointed questions and a far-reaching critique of exclusionary church policies along with positive, practical advice and wisdom for moving the church forward.

Within the unfolding saga of American Protestantism's grappling with issues of LGBT inclusion, Philip Wogaman's protest stands as a significant milestone. Beyond the initial impact that his action has seen, Wogaman has offered a real gift to the church with this wise and detailed account of the thinking that informs his witness."

—Mark Achtemeier, author of *The Bible's Yes to Same-Sex Marriage: An Evangelical's Change of Heart*

"Faithfulness to one's ordination includes bearing witness to the radical grace of God. So argues renowned pastor and ethicist J. Philip Wogaman. However, after sixty years of ministry, Wogaman realized—regretfully—that surrendering his own ordination was the particular act of faithful witness to which he was being called. Not merely a book about sexuality and church conflict, this is a profound meditation on the theological, ethical, and pastoral meaning of ordination; on the cost of discipleship; and, ultimately, on which version of Christianity we will choose to inhabit in the days to come."

—William Stacy Johnson, Arthur M. Adams Professor of Theology, Princeton Theological Seminary, and author of *A Time to Embrace: Same-Gender Relationships in Religion, Law, and Politics*

"I encourage anyone engaged in the Christian debate about sexuality to read this book. Using ordination as a lens, Dr. Wogaman invites us to look with him and to join in a reasoned, biblical conversation. As I read the book, I kept asking 'How am I like that? and 'How am I different from that?' Good conversation! He acknowledges the good faith of those with whom he disagrees, and that provides a context for faithful life together."

—F. Belton Joyner Jr., author of *Being United Methodist in the Bible Belt: A Theological Survival Guide for Youth, Parents, and Other Confused United Methodists* and *United Methodist Questions, United Methodist Answers*

"In his trademark clear and disarmingly accessible style, Dr. Phil Wogaman outlines the theological, ethical, and pastoral framework that undergirds both his decision to surrender his clergy credentials in 2017 and his sixty years in ordained ministry. We receive in this timely volume a deeply personal vision of Wogaman's own call and evolving ministry. We also receive insight into the painful decision to step outside the circle of ordained clergy to be in solidarity with those who are kept outside that circle as the result of 'bad church law.' I was in the room the day Rev. Wogaman took this step and give thanks for his thoughtful, powerful witness for LGBTQ equity and justice. Furthermore, I am honored to serve the congregation he led through the process of becoming fully and openly welcoming to LGBTQ people over twenty years ago. This book, like Phil Wogaman, is a gift to the church."

—Ginger E. Gaines-Cirelli, Senior Pastor, Foundry United Methodist Church

"Church arguments about same-sex love can seem like endless repetitions of familiar points. But at the heart of this book is something new: the practical, theological reasoning of a respected minister in deciding to surrender his ordination in response to his denomination's refusal to ordain faithful gay and lesbian Christians to ministry. J. Philip Wogaman does not argue for a general principle. He does not demand that others follow his lead. His argument is more personal and particular. And it is in the particulars that this book matters most; for it is on the rough, particular ground of reality that discipleship comes alive."

—Ted. A. Smith, Associate Professor of Preaching and Ethics, Candler School of Theology, Emory University

"Philip Wogaman's *Surrendering My Ordination* is a deeply thoughtful challenge to The United Methodist Church and to any church that fails to recognize the fullness of God's grace, the ethical challenge of 'bad church law,' and the demand to care for those who are being systemically and perpetually hurt. Wogaman places the whole conversation within the theology, ethics, and pastoral dimensions of ordination. He explains why he surrendered his ordination but also adds texture to theologies of ordination, ethical decision-making, and the church's ministry. His book is personal but not self-serving; it places Phil Wogaman's story at the center but without making the story about him. This story is about God and the church, about faithfulness and ethical decisions, about the pastoral care of all those who are being hurt. The focus is on sharing God's love and the community's love for the sake of justice and compassion and, more profoundly, for the sake of God."

— Mary Elizabeth Moore, Dean and Professor of Theology and Education, Boston University School of Theology

SURRENDERING MY ORDINATION

SURRENDERING MY ORDINATION

Standing Up for Gay and Lesbian Inclusivity in The United Methodist Church

J. Philip Wogaman

WJK WESTMINSTER
JOHN KNOX PRESS
LOUISVILLE · KENTUCKY

© 2018 J. Philip Wogaman

First edition
Published by Westminster John Knox Press
Louisville, Kentucky

18 19 20 21 22 23 24 25 26 27—10 9 8 7 6 5 4 3 2

All rights reserved. No part of this book may be reproduced or transmitted in any form
or by any means, electronic or mechanical, including photocopying, recording, or by
any information storage or retrieval system, without permission in writing from the
publisher. For information, address Westminster John Knox Press, 100 Witherspoon
Street, Louisville, Kentucky 40202-1396. Or contact us online at www.wjkbooks.com.

Scripture quotations from the New Revised Standard Version of the Bible are copy-
right © 1989 by the Division of Christian Education of the National Council of the
Churches of Christ in the U.S.A. and are used by permission.

Book design by Sharon Adams
Cover design by Barbara LeVan Fisher, www.levanfisherdesign.com

Library of Congress Cataloging-in-Publication Data

Names: Wogaman, J. Philip, author.
Title: Surrendering my ordination : standing up for gay and lesbian
  inclusivity in the United Methodist Church / J. Philip Wogaman.
Description: First edition. | Louisville, Kentucky : Westminster John Knox
  Press, 2018. | Includes bibliographical references. |
Identifiers: LCCN 2018012535 (print) | LCCN 2018029984 (ebook) | ISBN
  9781611648812 (ebk.) | ISBN 9780664264178 (pbk. : alk. paper)
Subjects: LCSH: United Methodist Church (U.S.)--Clergy. | Ordination--United
  Methodist Church (U.S.) | Homosexuality--Religious aspects--United
  Methodist Church (U.S.) | United Methodist Church (U.S.)--Doctrines.
Classification: LCC BX8345 (ebook) | LCC BX8345 .W64 2018 (print) | DDC
  262/.1476--dc23
LC record available at https://lccn.loc.gov/2018012535

Most Westminster John Knox Press books are available at special quantity discounts
when purchased in bulk by corporations, organizations, and special-interest groups.
For more information, please e-mail SpecialSales@wjkbooks.com.

To Bishop Joseph H. Yeakel
with many thanks

A charge to keep I have,
a God to glorify
. . . .
To serve the present age,
my calling to fulfill;
O may it all my powers engage
to do my Master's will.

—Charles Wesley (1762)

Contents

Acknowledgments

I was greatly moved by receiving a message of support from the editors of my longtime publisher, Westminster John Knox Press, soon after surrendering my ordination—and by later receiving their invitation to write this book. They have been helpful all the way. I am particularly grateful to Dan Braden, my principal editor, for his thorough care and wise counsel. More than a technical editor, Dan has the mind of a theologian and ethicist.

Several people have supported me throughout this endeavor. That includes the Revs. Mary Kay Totty of Dumbarton United Methodist Church, Ginger Gaines-Cirelli and Dawn Hand of the Foundry UMC, and Don Fado, longtime friend and retired California minister. My daughter, Jeanie, and brother, Tom, offered much support, as did Carolyn, my wife and loving companion of sixty-one years. These are the only persons I spoke to prior to surrendering my ordination, and they have been supportive ever since.

Subsequent to that action I've received much encouragement from people near and far—and enough criticism to help keep my feet on the ground. I wish I could name them all here.

But I think the book is more about T. C. Morrow and other highly competent candidates for ordination who've been

excluded than it is about me. I'm much impressed by how
T. C. has continued to respond with grace and perseverance. I
look forward to the time when she is finally ordained, knowing that in the meantime she is exercising ministry in the real
sense of that word. That is also true of Joseph Heath-Mason,
whose candidacy was not presented to the conference at the
same time as T. C.'s and for the same reason.

While thanking others, I know that any flaws in this book
are my own responsibility, not theirs.

Introduction

*T*his book explains the decision I made in May 2017 to give up my ordination in The United Methodist Church. It was entirely my own decision. I had been an ordained minister for sixty years, so this was no small matter. Let's be clear about what this decision did *not* mean. It did not mean that I was leaving the church, not even the United Methodist part of the church. I had been a Methodist since birth and baptism. My father was an ordained minister, so I grew up in a parsonage home as a preacher's kid. My decision was not a rejection of this heritage or an abandonment of the church. By my act I became a lay member of a local congregation.

Giving up my own ordination was not an act of disapproval of the idea of ordination itself. I know there are a few branches of the Christian church that do not have ordained clergy—I think especially of most of the Society of Friends (Quakers). But there are sound reasons for the church to have an ordained clergy, which I explore later.

By giving up my ordination, I was not urging or suggesting that others should follow my example. In fact, as I shall make clear, I pleaded with other clergy *not* to do so—again, for reasons I explain later.

I remain loyal to the church—both The United Methodist Church and the wider ecumenical church. As a lay member, now I understand that in the broadest sense all church members are ministers, whether or not they are ordained.

So why was I prompted to give up ordination after all these years and despite these loyalties?

My formal statement when I gave up my ordination had to be brief, just two or three minutes. I feel that all those who have been influenced by my ministry deserve a full account of my decision, and that is what this book is all about.

Here I lay out my understanding of what ordination means—and what it doesn't mean.

I see the meaning of ordination in three connections. First, what does it mean theologically? Second, what does it mean ethically? Third, what does it mean pastorally? Each of these dimensions was involved in my decision. Each has to be explored.

At bottom, the deep meaning of ordination is closely tied to our understanding of the church itself. You could almost say that ordination helps to define the nature of the church.

One other point must be clear at the outset. Whatever we may say about its theological significance, the church is a human institution. At its best, the church is inspired by deep faith and long legacies of faithful tradition. But it is still imperfect. Its members and clergy are all flawed human beings, although the church and its members are not merely sinners: our humanity has been touched by divinity, our faithlessness by a grounding in faith. By giving up ordination I was not prompted by some kind of ecclesial perfectionism. I was not rejecting the church for its imperfections but rather seeking to make it better.

In part 1, as a way to set the stage for explaining why I gave up my ordination, I explore the theological, ethical, and pastoral meanings of ordination and the process through which the church designates some persons for ordained ministry. Then, in part 2, I speak of my sixty years of ordained ministry and explain my difficult and somber decision to relinquish my ordination. I conclude with what this means to me and offer a reflection on the way forward for the church.

PART 1

The Meaning of Ordination

*W*hat does ordination mean? By giving up ordination, what is it that I have given up?

Here in part 1, I explore the meaning of ordination in three dimensions: theological, ethical, and pastoral. Very positive things can be said about each of these. But before exploring these meanings of ordination, I wish to disavow what is often considered the most important meaning of all: the idea that ordination confers special God-given powers on the minister or priest.

Major segments of worldwide Christianity have held that by giving or withholding the sacraments, the eternal destiny of an individual is substantially if not decisively affected. The priest or minister makes that decision, not arbitrarily but on the basis of objective criteria. I thought of that one day when attending the memorial Mass of a good friend and ecumenical colleague. The presiding bishop made clear that those who were not practicing members of that branch of Christianity must not receive the sacramental bread and wine. Nothing was said to imply that those of us who had been excluded would be denied eternal salvation. But at least we would not be allowed to partake of a sacrament that would be very helpful to us in the eyes of God. A priest, by virtue of his (always his, not her) ordination, had the power to make that decision. The scriptural basis used by some to support such a view is contained in Mark 16, where Jesus is reported as sending out his disciples to proclaim the gospel, saying that those who do not believe will be condemned. I just do not believe ordination confers such power. Even if one wishes to take such words literally, nothing is said there about ordination, much less about the Eucharist.

Of course, insofar as the faithful *believe* the priest or minister has such divinely instituted authority, ordination does confer a kind of institutional power. If I believe it, the word of the priest or minister will greatly affect my attitudes and actions. That is power. But to attribute it to God is more than a stretch.

And ordination is not something that should be reserved for men only, thus excluding half the human race. Actually, a majority of present-day Christians belong to churches that still reserve ordination to men. Sometimes exclusion is defended on the basis that Jesus' disciples were all men. Whether or not that is true I will leave to biblical scholars. But, again, to use that as a basis for exclusion of women smacks more of cultural bias than of theological principle. Indeed, would you use such logic to say that only Jews should be ordained because all of Jesus' disciples were Jews?

In part 1, I set forth some very positive aspects of ordination, in a theological perspective, an ethical perspective, and a pastoral perspective.

Chapter 1

Theological Meaning of Ordination

Among the several passages often cited as scriptural bases for ordination are accounts in Matthew 28:19–20 and Mark 16:15–18, which speak of how the post-resurrection Jesus sent his disciples forth to proclaim the good news. Without exploring the literal historicity of these passages, they plainly suggest that those who are called to discipleship are to represent Christ. While this does not in any direct sense refer to subsequent ordination practices, it does help us understand that the deep theological meaning of ordination is that some in the church have been set apart in a special way to represent Christ. A United Methodist statement on ordination declares that "through ordination and through other offices of pastoral leadership, the Church provides for the continuation of Christ's ministry, which has been committed to the church as a whole" (*Book of Discipline,* par. 303). A Disciples of Christ document on ministry conveys the point in these words: "In recognizing God's call to particular individuals, the Church designates persons 'to represent to the Church its own identity and calling in Jesus Christ.' . . . Authority and blessing to perform this ministry are celebrated in Ordination and Commissioning." Similar views are expressed by other Christian denominations.

Called to Represent Christ

Theology is, virtually by definition, God-centered. To be ordained is, in some sense, to be a representative of God. If the ordained are called to be representatives of Christ on earth, that means to be a representative of God, as understood through Christ. But who is this Christ whom the ordained are called to represent? Christ is viewed in a variety of ways by different Christians and their churches. The problem is almost like the different ways in which artists through the ages have sought to represent Jesus visually—there being no existing likenesses of Jesus from his own time.

By representing Christ, are we thinking primarily of his commandments, which are presumed to be of divine origin? That is suggested by the Matthew passage that directs the disciples to teach those to whom they are sent "to obey everything that I have commanded you" (28:20). That seems to portray Christ as divine lawgiver. Of course law has its place. But to think of the ordained as relaying the laws of Christ to others is but a step away from legalism: law, to be obeyed for its own sake. Doesn't representing Christ push us to a deeper level?

What about the teachings of Jesus about the nature of God and the spiritual blessings that come through the teachings? Think, for example, of the familiar parable of the Prodigal Son. The prodigal's father expresses the love of God that is constant despite human sinfulness. Or the teaching of Jesus in which God is portrayed as caring even for the fallen sparrow—and all the more for human beings. Such teachings seem far removed from a spirit of legalism. Even Jesus' reference to the great commandment to love God and neighbor bespeaks love itself as the central meaning of life.

Perhaps the apostle Paul has drawn us to a meaning of Christ that is more than Jesus' own specific teachings, important as they are.

For Paul, the cross is central. Jesus not only taught about love, he also accepted a horrendous death as an expression of love. Christ died for us. How is that so?

The substitutionary theory of the atonement is one explanation. According to this theory, God has been so offended by disobedient humanity that we should all suffer eternal punishment. That requires a sacrifice, given to God, that is greater than our sin. The freely given death of Jesus satisfies divine justice so that we can be forgiven.

That theory is but one of several and is not universally accepted by Christian churches. A problem with it is the depiction of God as being more concerned about divine justice than divine love. Put differently, it suggests that God's grace is in the service of law (helping us to understand and obey it) rather than law in the service of grace (enabling us to be more disciplined in our faithful response to God's free gift of love). Paul speaks of how we are "justified" not by works of the law but by faith in the free gift of God's grace through Christ. Paul's words are subject to multiple interpretations, but one thing stands out: We cannot, by what we do, *earn* salvation. Nobody is capable of being perfectly righteous. Paul doesn't say this, but one could explain the irony of relying on earning God's favor through obedience to God's law in this way: we are motivated by self-centeredness, not by love of God and love of fellow humanity.

Throughout their history, Christian churches have sought to understand and explain the complex meanings of God's grace. And yet, the simple point is that God, through Christ, has expressed a love that transcends human imperfection. By representing Christ, an ordained minister seeks to draw people into God's grace. By representing Christ, the ordained minister seeks to represent God. In Christ, the nature of God is revealed as love.

That is basic. But while saying that the essential nature of God is revealed in Christ, we remember that there is much more to God than can be encompassed in such a statement. God, understood as the center and source of all being, vastly exceeds human understanding. We sing "How Great Thou Art," little grasping just how great God really is.

Cosmic science has helped us explore the unfathomable vastness of the universe. By current NASA accounts, there seem to be as many as two trillion galaxies, containing on average some 100 billion stars. That is two trillion times 100 billion stars—and who knows how many planets, and of those, how many planets like ours with the possibility and actuality of human life? Jesus, in his era two thousand years ago, could not have grasped the factual dimensions of the universe. He did know, with the psalmist, that God's glory is "above the heavens" and that "the moon and the stars" have been established by God. And Jesus understood, in terms beyond the words of Psalm 8, that the God who has created everything has intimate, caring relationship with humankind.

Being ordained does not mean attaining an intellectual grasp of everything; it does mean representing Christ, who preeminently represented the God of all that is. And, above all, the God of everything is especially defined by love.

Representing the Church

It is the church that ordains those who are called out to represent Christ. The church, metaphorically understood as the body of Christ, is the enduring institutional expression of Christ's continuing reality among us. Those who are ordained by the church are thus a visible expression of the nature of the church. Ideas about what that means vary among denominations, and even within denominations, but they all are saying, in effect, that an ordained minister represents the nature of the church. That can be spoken of sociologically in this way:

So-and-so, one of our ordained ministers, represents who we are as a church. The ordained represent that to all within the church and to those who are not. Isn't it often the case that nonmembers generally consider an ordained minister to be a fit example of what the church is all about? The church, in effect, is judged by the perception one has of those whom the church has set forth as ordained.

We see this in a broader sense in relation to those who are designated by other religious bodies (Judaism, Islam, Buddhism, etc.) as representing the essential character of those spiritual communities. A Jewish rabbi, for instance, is typically regarded as a fit representative of the Jewish tradition, be it Orthodox, Conservative, or Reform. Essentially, the rabbi is a scholar and interpreter of the tradition, despite the many internal disagreements among rabbis about what the tradition means. A Muslim imam is one who leads in the prayers and often is taken as an authentic representative of what Islam is all about, again despite considerable differences among imams and among the various branches of Islam. Buddhism has no recognized clergy, per se, but its monks and spiritual guides are taken to be dependable guides and mentors to followers seeking to grow toward enlightenment. People who are outside these and other faith communities generally treat such leaders as authentic representatives of what the community is all about. So it is with ordained Christian clergy who, as representatives of particular church denominations, help outsiders and unordained believers alike to grasp the meaning of the church.

I believe that belongs to the fundamental meaning of ordination. An ordained minister is called to be a representative of the church, which represents Christ, who represents the God who is in all, and through all, and above all. That is a very large spiritual responsibility resting on the shoulders of those who have been ordained.

Thinking Theologically

An ordained minister is rightly expected to be able to interpret the faith theologically. This entails several important things.

First of all, it is to be able to distinguish between what is essential to the faith, what is important but open to debate, and what is not so important.

In Roman Catholic theological circles, that distinction is often presented as the difference between dogma and lesser theological teachings. I use the word "dogma" here cautiously because of negative connotations most people have about narrow-minded beliefs. When we speak of somebody as being "dogmatic" that is what we often mean: somebody who clings to absolute views regardless of evidence and in face of disagreements. But dogma has a higher meaning: those beliefs that are essential to the very nature of the faith and the church. An ordained minister must have some grasp of that.

So, in terms set forth above, the grandeur and grace of God are dogmatic affirmations. It is inconceivable that a Christian church could consider the reality of God as inconsequential or even open to debate.

The nature of God can be viewed in very different ways; churches and individual Christians express significant differences. For example, a church could be committed to a very judgmental and legalistic view of God and Christ, in sharp contrast with the views, expressed above, that God, seen through Christ, is defined by caring love. Such differences will be reflected in how ordination is established and viewed. Even to speak of God as grace or caring love can be empty abstractions unless they are intelligently fleshed out. Many, perhaps most, theologians today have concluded that theological thought is largely (if not entirely) metaphorical. Using words and concepts drawn from human experience, theological views express a reality beyond themselves. The word "love" has all sorts of human connotations, ranging from sexual attraction to self-giving concern for others.

It may help us to think theologically as we explore different theological entry points.

Theological Entry Points

A theological entry point can be described as some aspect of theology that helps illuminate the meaning of the basic affirmations of Christian faith—the Christian dogmas, as I used the term above. Here are several possible, and I think useful, entry points.

Covenant. Basic to both Jewish and Christian faith traditions, covenant is the relationship of humanity with God and the derivative relationships among human beings. God, through the ancient Hebrews, has established a covenant with the people of Israel. Sometimes viewed in more narrow terms as God's covenant with a chosen people, the term "covenant" was broadened even prior to Christ. That relationship between God and humanity is basic to our understanding the meaning of our lives. Christian churches have often characterized themselves as covenantal communities—faith communities that exist in and for their covenant with God. It is the meaning of the church and of the lives of people.

Heresy. This is another of those loaded words that turn off so many Christians. Given the history of how so-called heretics have been persecuted, even burned at the stake, I can see why people are reluctant to label anything as heresy. But if heresy means views and movements that are in direct conflict with the essence of the faith—the dogmas—this may be a useful starting point. Idolatries are by definition heretical, if we think of idolatry as worshiping something that is anything less than God. Many of the theological struggles reported in Hebrew Scriptures have to do with conflicts between YHWH and lesser deities. When Moses descended from Mount Sinai and discovered his fellow Israelites worshiping a golden calf they had made, he treated this as a fundamental denial of the God who had brought them out of captivity in Egypt. When Elijah condemned the prophets of Baal, he found a way to demonstrate to the people that the Baal objects of worship were powerless in the presence of the true God. When Jews and Christians refused to worship the Roman emperors, it was because they regarded that worship as such a fundamental denial of faith in the true God that they could not even go through the motions. Idolatry is the stuff of heresy.

In our own era, heresy has sometimes been dominant in human culture. Adolf Hitler's Nazism leaps to mind. It entailed deification of Aryan racial characteristics and utterly rejected Jews and racial minorities, along with other persons considered to be of no value. That was so blatantly contrary to Christian faith that Dietrich Bonhoeffer and others felt it necessary to create a Confessing Church, made up of people who rejected such a complete denial of authentic Christian faith. The German Christian movement, which went along with Hitler, represented a majority of the Christians in Germany. Those of the Confessing Church may have been a small minority, but their protest was against real heresy.

The heresy of racism has not been restricted to Germany's Third Reich. It was fundamental to the institution of slavery in the United States. Pre–Civil War disputes among Christians over slavery clearly, at least in retrospect, were about the heresy of racism. And many subsequent intra-Christian conflicts in Reconstruction America and apartheid South Africa centered around whether black people could be regarded as fully human. Again, it was a question of heresy. I recall interacting with a young official of the South African embassy in Washington, DC, over exactly that point.

A Dutch Reformed Christian, this South African probably represented a majority of the white South African members of his church in treating apartheid as the will of God.

We'll treat more such questions in the next chapter on the ethical meaning of ordination, but I repeat here that there are views of Christian faith that are rightly rejected as heretical.

Creation. This entry point emphasizes that the whole of existence has its origin in the creative purposes of God. This does not necessarily mean that God intended every specific aspect of creation to exist (mosquitoes and all). It does mean that God created all of the potentialities that came into existence, along with many that have not. So when we look at the stars and planets, the rivers and oceans, the forests and mountains, all were possibilities that God created. That is true also of the myriad life forms, up to and including human beings. The beginnings of creation on earth are poetically characterized in the book of Genesis, with the interjections that God "saw that it was good." So, for what purpose?

In the part of his *Church Dogmatics* detailing the doctrine of creation, Karl Barth artfully puts it this way:

> Creation is the external—and only the external—basis of the covenant. It can be said that it makes it technically possible; that it prepares and establishes the sphere in which the institution and history of the covenant take place, that it makes possible the subject which is to be God's partner in this history, in short the nature which the grace of God is to adopt and to which it is to turn in this history.

Barth's way of understanding creation is instrumental: creation is what makes the covenant possible. As he puts it, covenant is the meaning of creation.

I like that way of putting it, particularly because it is such a good entry point into much thinking about Christian ethics. I have come to wonder, however, whether Barth had sufficient regard for creation as an intrinsic reality and not only an instrumental means to the covenant. Isn't there something about God's work of creation that is good in and of itself? Even in aspects of creation that are destined to pass away? What about the great beauty of so much of creation? It is there, in part, for our enjoyment. Is it not also there for God to enjoy? Doesn't the mutual enjoyment of the vast beauties of creation between God and humanity constitute much of the content, the substance, of our covenant with God?

Another point has to be registered. The doctrine of creation helps us guard against an overemphasis on the spiritual. Almost from the beginning of Christian history there was a tendency among some Christians (notably the gnostics) to regard the material world as little more than an impediment to the spiritual life. The material world was regarded by some as the creation of a malevolent being or, at best, as a neutral reality that gets in the way of our spiritual life. Such an essentially negative view of the material world has captivated some Christian movements through history. But the doctrine of creation emphasizes that creation is good and that creation embodies, however mysteriously, the long-run purposes of God.

Sin. The concept of sin includes the painful reality that so much of human life has been and is opposed to the loving covenantal purposes of God. It is an inescapable part of human existence, despite efforts to wish it away. Christians and their churches have often sought to identify particular sins, against which we are warned at our peril. There may well be particular acts and attitudes that can be characterized as identifiable sins. But the reality of this entry point cuts deeper. Sin can be understood as estrangement from God, as a turning away from the covenant, even as a rejection of God's love.

The doctrine of original sin has been, historically, an effort by Christian theology to grapple with this human tendency to reject the goodness of God, often self-destructively. Sometimes original sin was taken, literally, to be the inherited legacy of the disobedience by Adam and Eve of God's requirement not to eat the forbidden fruit. There is profound truth in this myth. The fruit was from the tree of the knowledge of good and evil. So the original sin was in the birth of the human conscience—our capacity to distinguish between good and evil. And, implicitly, our capacity to be attracted by evil.

Whatever one makes of that, I rather prefer Reinhold Niebuhr's understanding of original sin as the human self-centeredness that is an inevitable, though not necessary, aspect of our inability to trust that our significance as human beings can be entrusted to the reality beyond us. When we can fully trust God, we no longer have to rely simply on ourselves. We may have to struggle with that problem for a lifetime, but real faith is in our trust of God. From a theological point of view, that is a part of the meaning of Christ for us. When we trust that the love of Christ for us is a disclosure of the nature and purposes of God, then we no longer have to "save ourselves" through self-centeredness.

I address issues of ethics more in the next chapter, but here we can see that the essence of sin is any attitudes, acts, or practices that stand in the way of receiving the grace of God. God's grace is always there. We don't earn it; we couldn't if we tried. But while God's love is constant, we can create barriers making it difficult to receive the greatest gift of all. To use a human metaphor, it is a bit like teenagers who feel alienated from their parents who, all the while, love them totally. The problem is not the withdrawal of the parents' love; it is the barriers on the teenager's side. Some of that separation is probably necessary for a child to gain mature identity. In any case, we are not to blame God for sin. Nor can we unambiguously label particular attitudes or acts as "sins" without seeing this in the ultimate divine-human perspective.

Freedom. In his Letter to the Galatians, Paul emphasizes the freedom we have in Christ. That is worth noting as another theological entry point. In part, it helps us understand why God tolerates human evils and injustices. Sometimes Christians ask: How could God allow a horrendous evil to exist, such as the Nazi and Rwandan and later genocides in which whole populations of people were exterminated? Or other tragic events at a more personal level? Couldn't God have intervened? Who knows? But if God did intervene, wouldn't that reduce our humanity to being puppets on a string?

With Paul, being secure in our trust in God's love, we can act not out of fear but out of love. We are free to be what God intends us to be. We are not slaves to divine or human law but free and responsible human beings who can act lovingly and creatively. More about this later.

Ordination - as basis for representing church

Conclusion

So here we have something of a theological basis for ordination. It is not a position of status that confers special objective powers. It is a basis for representing the church, which represents Christ, who represents God. Ordination, in some way, is an announcement by the church that this person is a fitting representative of what the church is all about.

Any reader may well ask whether my act of giving up ordination was because of my rejection of these theological views. Absolutely not! My action, in large measure, was taken because I hold these views. But before getting into that, it is important to speak about the ethical and pastoral meanings of ordination.

Chapter 2

Ethical Meaning of Ordination

*T*here are two complementary aspects of ethics: motivation and decision. The first asks, What do we will? Do we will what is good? Immanuel Kant declared that the only thing that is unconditionally good is the good will. If we do not will the good, then we are not basically a moral person. The other aspect is, how do we know what is the good that we will? Without a good will, we may stumble upon doing something good, almost by accident as we act for other reasons. But if we are moral persons who wish to do good, that fact will not assure that what we do is actually good. A good person may do bad things, not out of an evil will but because of mistaken judgment.

Those who concentrate only on the motivation side tend to assume that a good person will, by intuition, always get it right. And often they do get it right. But really good people can do really bad things through mistaken judgment. For instance, St. Catherine of Siena was, by all accounts, a real saint: ministering to plague victims, supporting ecclesial reforms, and so on. But she also urged on the crusaders. And good people through the centuries supported slavery and second-class status for women. Good people also need to study and think, using their minds to accomplish good things. Still, the starting point has to be the good will.

Both of these dimensions, motivation and decision, are part of the meaning of ordination.

The Moral Character of the Ordained

Nobody is perfect, but when the church chooses to ordain a person, that person's moral character is an important consideration. In the United Methodist ordination ritual, candidates for ordination are asked if they are "going on to perfection." The answer has to be yes. Then the follow-up question is, "Do you expect to be made perfect in this life?" Bishops have to come up with artful rationalizations of those questions, especially the second one! The first question has to do with your personal spiritual growth. If you aren't going toward perfection, where are you going? But the second question strains credulity.

While I once answered those questions affirmatively—as did all the other ordinands—I had few illusions about whether I really would become perfect in this life. Even John Wesley, the source of these questions, had to face criticism about such perfectionism. He didn't claim to be perfect himself, but he contended that a person could strive to be perfect by the very end of life. It helps a bit to know that Wesley's idea of perfection, perpetuated in the Methodist tradition, is defined by love. Perfection in love. My own problem with this is that perfection is a state of being, while love is dynamic and relational. The two are not a good fit.

Nevertheless, the church must expect its clergy to be persons of good and growing character. They must be people who truly represent what the church means about its being a community of love. That is a normal expectation of church members as well as outsiders. It hurts the church when clergy are involved in scandals, such as child abuse and exploitation of counseling relations. In recent years, the Roman Catholic

Church has come to know this all too well. I'm confident that a vast majority of Catholic priests have not abused children. And there have been problems among some Protestant clergy as well. In examining candidates for ordination, churches do well to consider issues of character carefully.

One especially dramatic illustration of the failure to do this was the infamous Rev. Jim Jones. A very charismatic leader, Jones attracted a large following; took them to Guyana, where he established Jonestown in an isolated forest setting; and ultimately led most of his followers to commit suicide to demonstrate what he considered worthy ends. Jones had started out, in Indiana, as a candidate for Methodist ordination. But that denomination has careful psychological examinations, which he was unable to pass. Switching to a denomination without such examinations, he passed and was ordained. (The other denomination has since revised its procedures!)

It remains true that nobody is morally perfect. But an important ethical meaning of ordination is that a person is good, as far as anybody can tell. In ministry, that will be demonstrated through acts of love and kindness in relationships. These qualities are important for all Christians, but those who are called to ordination should be exemplary.

Ethical Discernment and Decision Making

As we have said, even morally exemplary ordained ministers can be mistaken as they attempt to translate Christian faith into practical solutions to problems facing individuals, the church, and the world. We often face dilemmas, choices that must be made between competing goods or lesser evils. Seminary studies should help an ordained minister to confront issues with sophisticated discernment, but wise judgment can prove elusive. One is tempted to retreat into reliance on intuition alone, or even to feel that complex practical issues are not the business of church and ministry. But ordination is based on the expectation that a minister can provide helpful guidance, knowing that ethical issues matter.

An important reason for this is that the way human culture and institutions in the wider society are formed will lead us to do good things or bad things as we live normal lives. The social gospel theologian Walter Rauschenbusch had a succinct way of putting this. An unchristian society is one in which good people are forced to do bad things, while a Christian society is one in which bad people are led to do good things. He could have used America's racial segregation laws and customs of his era as an illustration. Just by leading a normal life in a segregated society, one sustains and reinforces the evils of racial discrimination. But, with passage of civil rights laws, a racist has to observe minority rights, like it or not. Customs and institutions matter. They can either undergird the moral life or obstruct it. Both kinds of institutions and customs are present most of the time in most societies.

The basic ethical problem is how to apply central values of the faith to the organization of our lives and society. A temptation for clergy is to counsel the faithful to do the right thing all the time. But life isn't always so simple. We face dilemmas when we confront choices of greater or lesser goods and greater or lesser evils and when we cannot have it both ways. Wise parents know that sometimes they have to choose between tolerating a child's misconduct or being too harsh in condemning it or pushing the child over the edge into something worse. Or a young person may have to choose between receiving immediate fulfillment in a line of work promising quick rewards or spending more years in preparation for work that will be more productive and fulfilling.

Political compromise entails decisions to accept imperfect social justice when the quest for perfection creates even greater injustice. The Christian just war doctrine was framed historically out of a huge dilemma that occurs when failure to engage in armed conflict may result in greater evils than the conflict itself. For example, would it have been better for the Allied countries not to militarily resist Hitler's Nazism so as to avoid the ravages of war? Would acceptance of genocide have been justified? That is doubtful. Of course, many wars, possibly most wars, are not so easily justified. The just war doctrine created a presumption against war; resorting to armed conflict had to bear the burden of proof.

Applied more generally, this approach to ethical decision making holds that we should apply our faith commitments as directly as possible, deviating from them or modifying them only for the sake of a greater good or a lesser evil. The question is where to place the burden of proof. I have developed this theme at greater length in other writings, but here I note its relevance to the question of ordination: First, candidates for ordination are not perfect. So the process of ordination involves weighing positives and negatives, greater and lesser degrees of moral virtue. A candidate for ordination, one who feels the call to ministry, can be presumed to be a sufficiently virtuous person unless there is enough evidence to the contrary. And second, a candidate for ordination should evince maturity of judgment.

Relating Values to Facts

Christians, and the adherents of other faiths, can derive ethical values more or less directly from the content of their faith. For example, love is central. The qualities of love singled out in the teachings of Jesus and in Paul's 1 Corinthians 13 depict loving-kindness in different forms. Through the faith, we are drawn into the love of God, expressing that love in our regard for fellow humanity. We are not to treat anybody as an enemy; everybody is loved by God and is to be regarded by us as a sister or brother. That is an incomparably important moral value. Similarly, this faith tradition considers the natural world to be the good creation of God and to be preserved and enhanced by human actions. Other values can be derived from the theological perspectives developed in the preceding chapter. But note: values derived from faith traditions still have to be worked out in the factual world. Facts are not the same thing as values, but they set limits and open up possibilities for translating the values into reality. Serious ethical decision making must include both the values we want to pursue and the factual context.

An illustration: All human life is valued as a gift from God. In a democracy, that translates into equality before the law and equal participation in determining the future of society, its laws and policies. But not all can vote. Why does a real democracy deny voting rights to six-year-old children? The fact is that young children are not yet mature enough, by virtue of experience and education, to be responsible voters. That factual judgment determines the extent to which the value of equal participation can be achieved. Prior to 1920, women were denied the vote in most states, based on long-standing factual judgments that proved to be totally false. Throughout history, marginalized groups, including racial and ethnic minorities, were denied equal privileges and subjected to slavery and crude forms of discrimination on the assumption, held by many, that persons in such groups were intellectually and even morally inferior. But factually it turns out the evidences of group inferiority are a direct result of people being denied opportunities, particularly in education. When equal opportunity was available, through civil rights laws and affirmative action programs, members of marginalized groups were able to demonstrate their factual equality. This has happened in the United States on an immense scale over the past fifty years.

Factual possibilities and limitations are important in almost every aspect of ethical decision making. Big debates over the morality of abortion depend largely on factual evidence of prenatal development. At what point, *factually*, is there enough development of the brain to conclude that in some rudimentary sense this fetus can be called a person? To some extent, pro-life and pro-choice adversaries implicitly rely on factual information.

Economic decisions, on both the personal and the wider social level, rely on factual data about how an economy works. Are the libertarians right, for instance, in their claims that the unimpeded, even unregulated, market will invariably enhance the economic benefits of all—in some version of Adam Smith's celebrated claims about the "invisible hand"? And is it true that most people receiving governmental welfare benefits are seeking to avoid work and to game the system? Or are all such economic assumptions deeply flawed? Are state economies with strong governmental programs to provide a safety net better forms of human community? Questions of this kind are largely determined by the adequacy of factual information.

One can think of countless areas of life in which responsible ethical decision making depends not just on values alone but also on greater factual information. Put in traditional ethical language, our ends are the values we pursue, but facts largely determine the means necessary to achieve them. The deep relationship between values and facts, ends and means, will emerge in significant ways in discussions of homosexuality during the second part of this book. It remains true, however, that there can be very sharp differences about both values and facts.

An ordained minister cannot be expected to be an expert about all this. She or he should be able to articulate the ultimate value issues with clarity and to note what kinds of facts must be pursued rigorously. The church as a whole can provide opportunities for collective decision making that combine solid theological and ethical insight with factual expertise.

The church's ordained clergy have a vital role to play in this. Often lay members have backgrounds of factual expertise that are very important in developing responsible church teaching on the issues of the day—both those that are more personal and the ones involving wider social contexts. An environmental scientist can illuminate the meaning of trends of climate change and the role of human activity. A farmer can help us understand agricultural issues. Health care professionals can illuminate medical issues. Economists can speak to the likely outcomes of different economic policies. And so on. Lay experts cannot, on the basis of facts alone, determine the moral issues, since values and facts both matter. But the interaction of experts with theologians and ethicists can be very productive, both at local church and denominational and ecumenical levels. Ordained clergy can be especially helpful in fostering such interdisciplinary conversation about ethical issues.

The Church's Social-Ethical Teaching

At the denominational level, The United Methodist Church and other denominations have developed many statements and resolutions on moral issues. In the 2016 *Book of Resolutions*, numbering 873 pages, some two hundred statements and resolutions adopted by the UM General Conference are laid out. An ordained minister is not expected to agree with everything contained there—I doubt that very many clergy have even read them all. But because these are official declarations of their church, ordination conveys a responsibility to take them seriously. This is similar to Roman Catholic response to papal encyclicals. The papal statements are not regarded as infallible, but as declarations by the head of the church they are considered to be worthy of careful consideration. An ordained Protestant minister who voices disagreement with an official denominational teaching should be prepared to indicate clear reasons for the disagreement.

I can add, just in passing, that the political process through which a statement is adopted at a UM General Conference sometimes detracts from its credibility as a serious expression of deep Christian values. As a delegate to four UM General Conferences, I have sometimes been troubled by how narrow interests and cultural biases can determine outcomes. Still, on the whole I find most of the contents of the *Book of Resolutions* to be thoughtful guidance, grounded in the faith.

That is even more the case with UM Social Principles. These are more general statements about different spheres of human life. They often form the basis for more detailed teachings of statements and resolutions. As I write, efforts are under way to refine and condense the Social Principles. As it is, they need to be taken even more seriously by clergy, and local churches are expected to review them periodically.

But even the Social Principles are not beyond criticism. I note, for example, some conflicted teaching. At one point, in dealing with issues of war and peace, the Social Principles strike almost a pacifist tone by flatly declaring that "we believe war is incompatible with the teachings and example of Christ. We therefore reject war as an instrument of national foreign policy." At another point we read that "some of us believe that war, and other acts of violence, are never acceptable to Christians. We also acknowledge that many Christians believe that, when peaceful alternatives have failed, the force of arms may regretfully be preferable to unchecked aggression, tyranny, and genocide." Having been involved in some of the debates over this issue, I can attest that neither statement reflects the deepest views of all delegates. The end result has been a kind of recognition of principled disagreement.

Conclusion

The ethical meaning of ordination is partly that those who are set apart for ordination by the church must be persons of good, though not perfect, character, and that they should strive to be thoughtful in their ethical teaching. They should be helpful guides to fellow Christians on the issues of the day, and they should represent the best of the church's teaching to people who are not a part of the church. By clear articulation of the ethical implications of the faith, they can help demonstrate how Christian faith can be a credible basis for the organization of personal and social life.

Back to the original question of this book: has the ethical meaning of ordination led me to give up ordination? Certainly not! My decision, to be discussed in part 2, was largely an outgrowth of my lifetime of study of Christian ethics and my efforts to better translate Christian ethics into practice.

Chapter 3

Pastoral Meaning of Ordination

*W*hen many people think of the meaning of ordination, the pastoral dimension is probably what leaps most readily to mind. Lay church members can often think of some pastor who has been especially important to them, both in periods of personal distress and in joyous times of celebration. In those meaningful personal relationships, the pastor represents the whole community.

When, after many years of seminary teaching, I was asked to become pastor of a Washington, DC, church, one anxiety stood out: How would I handle hospital visits? Would hospitalized parishioners consider it an intrusion for me, as a pastor, to show up at bedside? I laugh about that anxiety now. Exactly the opposite is what I discovered; I was more than welcomed. When the patient's eyes lit up, I don't think it was because of my charming bedside manner. It was because I represented the whole church of which the parishioner-patient was a member. I would sometimes speak of it this way: "The whole church would like to be here, but they couldn't all fit in this room. So they sent me to say how much they care for you and pray for your speedy recovery." There was a bit of hyperbole in such a greeting—which we both understood. But the point was still truthful. I had been set aside, through ordination, to be a representative of the whole church in expressing the faith community's mutual caring.

Caring for People

My own seminary classes in pastoral care—now more than half a century ago—gave particular emphasis to models of psychological therapy. Some of that was helpful. But there was a note of professionalism about it that detracted from genuine caring. I have discovered through the years that you cannot be much of a pastor for people whom you do not, in some basic sense, really love. You want what is best for a person and seek to discover that with them. That doesn't mean telling somebody what they should or shouldn't do, but neither are you simply a bystander. There can be moments when you are very direct, but most of the time you are a listening presence.

People wonder sometimes what they should say when calling upon a family that has lost a loved one. But the point isn't what you need to say; it is that you are there. Words, if needed, will come. As an ordained minister, you are the visible presence of the whole church to comfort and sustain. Just being there is what matters most. For there is a real sense in which your being there embodies the presence of the whole church that has ordained you and sent you.

That is also true of other, more joyous occasions, including weddings and anniversaries and baptisms. The pastor's presence is that of the whole church. That, incidentally, is one reason why baptisms generally occur in the context of a worship service, in the presence of the entire congregation and not in an isolated place. While the pastor can represent the whole church in a different setting, it is all the better when the whole congregation is visibly present.

So pastoral care is more than a one-on-one exercise in therapy. It involves the whole church. During my years of ministry at Foundry United Methodist Church in Washington, DC, I borrowed a way of involving the whole church from a colleague. During a more informal part of a service, devoted to announcements and concerns, I would note when a parishioner was in hospital or suffering a bereavement or celebrating a wedding or other joyous event. I would then ask whether somebody in the congregation would be willing to make contact with those affected to say that we were thinking about them in a special way. I would wait until somebody raised a hand. I did make clear that this contact from the congregation was not a substitute for my own pastoral contact, and I certainly made this move only after receiving the permission of the people affected. This was a fairly large congregation, but such a move helped symbolize how we all belong to one another. In a limited sense, those who responded by making the contact were being "ordained," then and there, to minister on behalf of the congregation.

In a larger, more general sense, that is exactly what the denomination as a whole has done in ordaining its clergy, setting them loose to represent the church in ministry. An important part of selecting and preparing those called to ordination is the church's determination of their aptitude for this pastoral dimension of ministry. Do they have a pastor's heart? Nobody does perfectly, but this remains important.

Spiritual Leadership

There is, I believe, an even deeper dimension to the pastoral meaning of ordination, implied by the theological and ethical meanings we have already considered. That dimension is helping people to become more loving and to overcome things that make it more difficult for them to experience the grace of God. If sin is what stands in the way, then spiritual leadership illuminates both the wonder of God's love and the attitudes, values, and practices that obstruct our vision. We may be addicted to materialism or the quest for fame or power over others, little realizing how such idolatries obstruct the greater gift of love. Pastoral ministry is prophetic in that it helps people see things that stand in the way. I think of the prophetic as not simply condemning but as exposing the tragedy of sin as an obstacle to love.

Spiritual leadership is both personal and social.

In speaking of the personal, I recall a moment in one of our church's healing services. These services occurred weekly in a small chapel. They did not pretend to offer cures for diseases; the healing being sought was usually at an emotional or spiritual level. We began with the Eucharist. Following Communion, anybody could come forward, kneel at the altar rail, and speak to one of the clergy—under circumstances guaranteeing privacy. One evening, I wasn't really in the mood for any of this. But a young man came forward, knelt before me, and tearfully poured out his heart in such a way that I instantly felt his pain. He voiced a deep sense of unworthiness, a feeling that his life no longer mattered to him or to anybody else. I couldn't know all the details of his life: Had he failed to live up to the expectations of others? Had he been unable to succeed vocationally or in relationships? Did he feel rejected by other people and by God? I couldn't know the details in that moment, though I sensed a basic level of integrity in him and he had, of course, come to this place in search of a better life. On instinct, I grasped his shoulders, and I spoke directly to him about how his life mattered to God and to the rest of us. I had a sense of pastoral connection in that moment, and I think he did too.

That is just one illustration of spiritual leadership on an individual level.

The Roman Catholic practice of confession, penance, and absolution helps make the personal level clear. The priest-confessor is, in effect, authorized by the church to diagnose different kinds of sin, as confessed by the penitent, and to prescribe forms of penance that will overcome the power of sin that separates one from God. So the priest is a representative of the church in its understanding of salvation. Protestant churches have done away with this practice, by and large, but the pastoral role of ordained clergy in helping people understand and resist the ravages of sin remains. Sometimes that must mean awakening a deeper sense of guilt; and sometimes it must challenge misplaced, inappropriate feelings of guilt, as I think it did in the incident related above.

Pastoral leadership can also occur in the wider context of a whole society. Martin Luther King's leadership in the civil rights movement was more than an effective political strategy. He saw clearly that the disease of racism is a huge obstacle to a people collectively experiencing God's grace. The march he led from Selma to Montgomery, Alabama, in 1965 was pivotal in enfranchising millions of African Americans who had systematically been deprived of the vote. At a deeper level it represented a spiritual outpouring and awakening by people of different faith communities to liberation from the tragedy of racism.

One dramatic pastoral moment occurred in the days before the march. Earlier attempts at conducting the march had been brutally turned back by Alabama police. Now, under court order, it was going to proceed with federal protection. King had appealed to people of goodwill from all over the country to come and be participants. Many came, including busloads of college-age people from California. Impatient with the spiritual dimensions of the movement, they sought to impose their particular understanding of the march upon others; and that night, in the usual gathering of protesters in the headquarters church, Brown's Chapel AME Church, the young people, with plenty of zeal yet little wisdom, domineeringly harangued the gathering. As an eyewitness to this event, I was struck when an elderly African American man (who I think was a pastor) stood in the chancel and spoke directly to the young people: "We don't know why you're here. Anybody can come. But if you are not here because of God, you don't belong." His words and his manner had an immediate effect in restoring the essentially spiritual character of the gathering and of the march itself. It was a pastoral moment. It was not just about political decision making for abstract political purposes but also about restoring the deeper meaning of inclusive national community.

King understood that this community even included the oppressing majority. In a certain sense, to be part of this majority was to be wounded spiritually without realizing it, perhaps even more than the victims of oppression; and partly because he understood this, Dr. King was for years the most important spiritual leader in this country.

Based on a more limited understanding of the pastoral meaning of ordination, I puzzled over what was meant when bishops, especially in the Catholic Church, issued "pastoral" letters to the faithful, or what the Second Vatican Council meant in referring to one of its key declarations as the Pastoral Constitution on the Church in the Modern World. Such messages are not about one-on-one counseling. They are attempts to define spiritual leadership, helping to illuminate the deeper purposes of God. The opening words of that declaration illustrate exactly its pastoral character: "The joys and the hopes, the griefs and the anxieties of the [persons] of this age, especially those who are poor or in any way afflicted, these are the joys and hopes, the griefs and anxieties of the followers of Christ. Indeed, nothing genuinely human fails to raise an echo in their hearts."

Of course, the church itself can create barriers to the full realization of the grace of God. Great church reformers, such as Martin Luther, John Calvin, and John Wesley, provided what was essentially pastoral leadership. To be ordained by the church can mean, ironically, that one is called to seek the spiritual healing of the church. That means that one is ordained to represent the church *insofar as* it embodies the reality of Christ, who expresses the depth of God's love. That can create dilemmas.

John Wesley, founder of Methodism, was an Anglican priest until his dying day. His purpose as spiritual leader of the Methodist movement was not to tear the Church of England apart but to draw it back to its deeper purposes. When his authority to preach to people for whom he had no parish responsibility was challenged, he insisted that his authority was from God. In response to one questioner, he famously replied, "I look upon all the world as my parish. . . . This is the work which I know God has called me to; and sure I am that His blessing attends it." Then, when Bishop Butler of Bristol (where Wesley had preached outdoors to large crowds) informed him, "You have no business here; you are not commissioned to preach in this diocese," Wesley replied that he must preach "the gospel wherever I am in the habitable world." He continued to assert that "being ordained a priest, by the commission I then received I am a priest of the Church Universal," and that if his preaching should break any human law "it will be time to ask, 'Shall I obey God or man?'" That came very close to direct ecclesial disobedience, although Bishop Butler took no disciplinary action.

Conclusion

Did I give up my ordination because I no longer accepted its pastoral dimension as an important meaning of ordination? Again, the answer is an emphatic *no*. That will become clear in part 2.

Chapter 4

The Process of Ordination

*D*ifferent denominations have processes of ordination that are unique to them, although the representational meanings discussed in previous chapters are more or less common to all. In some denominations, ordination is formally an action by the whole church; in some, it is done by an individual, local church; in others, it is a mixture of the two. Bishops of the Episcopal Church, who have this authority from the whole denomination, do the ordaining. In Baptist churches, by contrast, ordination is authorized and acted upon by a local church.

The United Methodist Church uses a long process that includes a personal sense of having been called, with careful screening by different layers of the church. Candidates, who have to be members in good standing of a local UM church, must contact the district superintendent to request admission to the candidacy process, be assigned a clergy mentor to help guide further progress, write a statement of why they have felt called to ordained ministry, be interviewed about that statement, be approved by the pastor-parish committee of their local church and by its charge conference, be approved by psychological examination, be examined and approved by the district committee on ordained ministry (which includes both clergy and lay members), attend and graduate from an approved theological seminary (normally a three-year program that follows receiving a bachelor's degree from an accredited college or university), be examined by the conference board of ordained ministry, be recommended for provisional conference membership by a three-fourths majority of that board, be approved by the clergy session of the annual conference by three-fourths majority vote, serve at least two years as a provisional member of the conference, then be approved again by the board and by the clergy executive session. The *Book of Discipline of The United Methodist Church* provides details for each of these stages and actions.

The vetting process for the designation of ordained United Methodist clergy is extensive!

The process includes two key aspects: first, the candidate's personal sense of calling; second, the confirmation of the candidate's calling by the church at different levels of the institution. So we have both subjective and objective aspects: the subjective feelings or belief of the candidate and the objective appraisal by the church. All of this underscores the reality that an ordained minister is a representative of the whole church. Moreover, the details provided in the United Methodist *Book of Discipline* underscore the theological, ethical, and pastoral meanings of ordination—if not precisely in the terms outlined in chapters 1, 2, and 3 above.

Another point is worth highlighting: lay members of the church participate at every level up to the more exclusive clergy executive session of the annual conference that gives final approval. That underscores how ordination is an affirmation by the whole church.

The process is a good deal more elaborate now than it was sixty years ago when I was ordained. Some of the changes may be desirable, others perhaps less so. When I entered the ordination process, every minister was first ordained a deacon—which could be done, under some circumstances, after only one year of seminary, and one could be ordained an elder after completing seminary—without the currently required two years of provisional service. The years of provisional service may be a good thing, but I rather regret loss of the two-stage ordination as deacon and then elder.

As it stands, United Methodist church law calls for a permanent deaconate, separate from the elders' order. Requirements for the two are comparable, and the process of qualifying is equally rigorous. One major difference, however, is that an elder is guaranteed an appointment with material support, while deacons must locate their own position, to which they are appointed by the bishop if the bishop approves. A deacon's work can be within the church (for example, as a church musician or administrator) or in some agency of service outside. An ordained deacon is a member of the clergy session of an annual conference and can be elected as a delegate to the General Conference.

While both deacons and elders are ordained for life, they can voluntarily relinquish their orders. Those who exercise this option then become lay members of a local United Methodist church of their choosing.

PART 2

Why I Gave Up Ordination

*T*o give up ordination, after sixty years, was not an easy decision! I deal with what prompted the decision in chapter 6. But, first, I provide a brief narrative account of those sixty years to give the reader a sense of what this meant to me. Chapter 6 gives an account of what actually happened, what immediately precipitated the move. Chapters 7–9 explore the meaning of this action, drawing upon the theological, ethical, and pastoral dimensions explored in part 1. A concluding chapter discusses how I believe the church can find a way out of its present impasse that largely prompted my decision.

I want to emphasize two things. I am not, here, rejecting The United Methodist Church.

I love this church. I have experienced its life on different levels and in many different places. I think immediately of many of its people, both lay and clergy, who affected my life for good. Moreover, I can affirm so much of the prophetic social witness of The United Methodist Church. On the whole, I believe this church has been a real force for good, both for its own members and in the wider world.

Second, I do not harbor animosity to those whose hurtful actions occasioned my move. We all see in a glass darkly, as Paul reminds us. I've had to learn and grow through the years, and I hope that process has not ended quite yet. We all need to love one another, both within and beyond the church, despite our differences.

Chapter 5

My Sixty Years
of Ordained Ministry

*T*his chapter is frankly autobiographical. The story of the years of my ministry prior to the surrender of my credentials will help to place that action in context.

I cannot honestly record any dramatic moment when God spoke to me directly about entering ministry, although there was a definite point of decision. I had grown up in a parsonage home, the son of a Methodist minister. That upbringing meant that I was no stranger to Methodist ministry, although childhood experience was doubtless superficial. In thinking about my own future, the ministry was always an attractive option, although I wanted to be sure that such a decision was not simply following in my father's footsteps—much as I loved and respected him. It had to be authentically my own decision.

The moment came at a Methodist youth summer camp just as I was finishing high school. The camp speaker, the Rev. Richard Dunlap, was one of those clergy who had a special gift for communicating with youth. I don't recall his making any particular pitch for his young listeners to consider ministry as a vocation, but somehow what he had to say spoke to my heart. And I decided then and there that, yes, this was the direction I should pursue. My sense of what that might mean was doubtless immature. But it set a trajectory that provided for growth in maturity and spiritual discernment. Was it a calling from God? Who's to say? God speaks to us in many different ways, and we can be led. I never had reason to doubt that this was the direction in which I was being led, although there have been so many twists and turns along the way.

Years of Preparation

I knew, of course, that years of preparation lay ahead. I had never doubted that I would go to college, but this decision helped define the form that education would take. After one year in a small junior college near my home in Safford, Arizona, I attended the (then) small College of the Pacific in Stockton, California. My studies there ran the gamut of liberal arts and social science courses, including the college's required Old and New Testament courses. I had to work my way through college, which, in the long run, gave me a better sense of the working world. Additionally, during my college years in Stockton I experienced the ethnic and economic diversity of that city. And I gained valuable leadership experience through student government.

After finishing college, I enrolled at Boston University School of Theology—then, as now, a very progressive seminary with much emphasis on social justice. (It had been Dr. Martin Luther King Jr.'s graduate school, although our years there barely overlapped.) My field work at the School of Theology included service as a YMCA youth director in Roxbury and as part-time minister to students at nearby Second Church of Boston. Ordained a deacon after one year of seminary (legally possible in those years), I served as co-pastor, with my brother-in-law, of the Methodist Church in Marlborough, Massachusetts. We had both gotten married the summer after our first seminary year and, with our new spouses, we settled into the large, rambling parsonage.

After graduation from the School of Theology, I began PhD studies, also at Boston University. My chosen field was social ethics, and my doctoral adviser was Dean Walter G. Muelder, an internationally recognized leader in the field. My choice of social ethics was partly academic, but it was also influenced by my involvement in social justice issues through the years. We had moved to Arizona (for my father's health) when I was eleven years old, and I had the benefit of a home in which social justice issues were addressed, including racial issues, migrant labor problems, and problems facing American Indians at an impoverished nearby reservation.

My doctoral study focused largely on racial issues, and my PhD dissertation addressed how to accomplish desegregation in all levels of the (then) Methodist Church. (The dissertation was published and sent to all delegates to the 1960 General Conference.) Doctoral study helped me better understand the deep relationship between theology, ethics, and practical engagement with social problems.

A Ministry of Teaching

Through most of my student years I fully intended to return to the Southern California–Arizona Annual Conference to become a pastor. But I began to wonder, as I neared completion of PhD study, whether I should consider teaching instead. After careful consideration, I and my wife, Carolyn, agreed to become missionaries to Cuba, where I would teach at its Union Theological Seminary. But that was in 1960, and the prospect fell through while we were studying Spanish in Costa Rica. By then the idea of a teaching ministry had taken hold, so we agreed to go back to my college alma mater in Stockton, where I would teach Bible and social ethics while leading a research program on church-state relations in California.

While I taught courses on social ethics, most of my work was with Old and New Testament. I had not done doctoral study on the Bible, but teaching introductory classes in Old and New Testament for five years proved to be an invaluable experience. The benefit was not so much from better grasp of technical issues of biblical scholarship, which I cheerfully leave to real experts, but from repeated review of the biblical narratives and teachings. I had studied Bible in college and seminary years, of course, but this teaching pushed me into a deeper grasp of profound scriptural treasures. In the long run, it was to draw me deeper into the theological meaning of Christian ethics. My work in ethics continued, including engagement with social issues such as the campaign against discrimination in housing.

In 1966 I was invited to join the faculty at Wesley Theological Seminary in Washington, DC. Carolyn and I readily accepted the change. For me, it was opportunity to concentrate in my field of social ethics and to do it in the nation's capital. During twenty-six years of teaching at Wesley, I helped to educate generations of future clergy, mostly United Methodists but also students from other denominations. Most were headed toward ordination, some were engaged in theological study with different career intent, and a few found in the course of their studies that ministry simply was not their real calling. For all, Washington was a superb environment for study of social ethics.

During those years I was able to do much more research and writing. One of my models for that work was the late Professor Georgia Harkness of the Pacific School of Religion, with whom I served on a couple of committees in California and whose books I found especially attractive.

Was this career pattern real ministry? Clearly, yes. The teaching itself was, one way or another, an exploration and communication of the faith. The years also involved a fair amount of preaching and teaching in churches in various parts of the country, pastoral engagement with students, and service to the connectional church at different levels.

Social Justice Activism

My years of ministry involved a lot of engagement with the social-ethical issues of the day. This began well before my ordination, even during student years. That included participating in efforts to foster greater inclusion of racial and ethnic minorities and Jews. Much of this was influenced by my home environment, with a mother and father who actively encouraged the struggle against racism in all its forms. My preacher-father voiced prophetic sermons (and was partly responsible for desegregating schools in an Arizona community). My participation in social justice causes was also prompted by direct observation of the plight of migratory workers—Steinbeck's "grapes of wrath"—and of the impoverished Cocopah tribe on a reservation near one of our Arizona hometowns. I don't recall feeling heroic about any of this; it just seemed to come naturally.

During my teaching years at the University of the Pacific, I, along with a number of other younger faculty members, formed the Stockton Fair Housing Committee to fight against housing discrimination. We participated in a campaign to create fair housing legislation. We were not successful at the time, but the campaign laid the groundwork for later laws. I recall that we younger faculty members supported Cesar Chavez's farm labor movement by helping to prevent shipment of grapes by an agricultural organization that resisted unionization. In 1965 I was among those who responded to

Dr. King's call for people to come to Selma for the march to Montgomery, Alabama. During the Wesley Seminary years, I, along with many others, became deeply involved in the anti-war movement. The list could go on. I want to emphasize that most of this just came naturally, without any sense of heroism. It was, to me, simply a part of what ministry is all about.

In light of the subject matter of this book, a reader might well ask at what point I became active in issues related to homosexuality. That is a fair question. In fact, I came to that rather late. During the decade or so after completing my doctoral studies in social ethics, I didn't pay much attention to those issues at all. If asked (which I rarely was), I'd have said that homosexuality was a form of emotional pathology or of sin or some mixture of the two—but I didn't want to be distracted by those issues from my focus on what I considered weightier issues. But during the mid-1970s or so, I found I couldn't as a teacher of ethics ignore those issues any longer. I studied the issues and, more importantly, I became better acquainted with gay and lesbian people and the hurt they were suffering at the hands of the church.

Serving the Connectional Church

From the beginning, my years as an ordained minister included considerable involvement with the church at connectional levels—that is, the church structures extending beyond the local church. I was often called upon to be a consultant to the Board of Church and Society (and its predecessor boards), located in Washington, DC. Earlier, I had been a member of the conference Board of Social and Economic Relations in Northern California. While at Wesley I was a member of the conference Board of Ordained Ministry for eight years, serving as president for four of those years. In 1980 I was asked to serve as chair of a general church committee seeking to negotiate an end to the Nestlé Company's infamous marketing of breast-milk substitutes in third-world countries—an effort that was ultimately successful. I was elected as a delegate to the General Conferences of 1988, 1992, 1996, and 2000, and to the jurisdictional conferences of 2004 and 2008. At each of these General Conferences I was actively engaged in the struggle to change policies affecting gay and lesbian people, including authoring the legislation in 1988 creating the Committee to Study Homosexuality. I served as a member of the church's General Council on Finance and Administration from 1996 to 2004 and on the Commission on Christian Unity and Inter-religious Concerns from 2004 to 2008.

These and other involvements at the conference and denominational levels were not just an ego trip; they involved hard but necessary work for the church. I mention them here to underscore that my institutional involvements with broad church structures and laws were not incidental. When I took the action described in the following chapter, I had a clear understanding of what it could mean.

The Foundry Years

In 1992, after service on the Wesley faculty for twenty-six years, I was asked by Bishop Joseph Yeakel to become senior minister of the Foundry United Methodist Church, also in Washington, DC. He anticipated a crisis in that centrally located downtown church and thought I would be able to deal with it. Founded in 1815, Foundry has played a key role in the religious life of the nation's capital throughout its two-plus centuries of service. When asked why I would leave a seminary faculty for that pastorate, I'd jokingly say that after decades of teaching future clergy, it was time for me to put up or shut up. The church did face many challenges during those years, including the crisis that Bishop

Yeakel anticipated. But those were wonderful years, and neither Carolyn nor I ever regretted the decision to go there.

Not incidentally, the church served a very diverse congregation, including people who had been rejected elsewhere and, in terms of status and class, parishioners ranging from the homeless to leading figures in Congress and even the president of the United States. It is and was a progressive church, challenging those who occupied its pulpit to make the gospel relevant both to individuals and to the collective life of the city and nation.

I have written mainly of my own professional involvements during my sixty years of ordained ministry, but in more ways than I can name my ministry was shared and supported by my wife, Carolyn. As noted above, we were married during my seminary years, which means that as of this writing we've been married for sixty-two years. Our decision to accept Bishop Yeakel's invitation to go to Foundry was fully shared. Carolyn had been a preschool teacher at the National Child Research Center in Washington and felt it was time to retire from that. She was interested in turning her attention to inner-city problems, and the Foundry challenge seemed a good way to become more involved. She then spent years as chair of the board of the Calvary preschool learning center, a program designed to reach and help Latino young people. That program evolved into a full-scale educational enterprise called Centronia. Even before the Foundry years, she was instrumental in forming an innovative summer program for children from a number of suburban and inner-city churches conducted for fifteen years in Washington's Rock Creek Park. As parents, she and I raised four children, and she had to do a whole lot of the heavy lifting.

The time came when the Foundry years had to end, because I had reached the then mandatory retirement age of seventy. Perhaps it was about time anyway. It had been a wonderful experience, but it was time to turn the responsibility over to others. But ministry doesn't end with retirement. A couple of years later I was asked to be interim president of Iliff School of Theology in Denver, which I served from 2002 to 2004. Then the bishop of Nebraska asked me to be interim pastor of a church in Omaha. And so on, with more teaching and writing and involvements with the church. I recognized that ordination is a lifetime commitment.

But there came a point, which is what this book is about, when even that commitment had to be set aside for sufficient cause. When the time came, I didn't give up my credentials because of the meaning of ordination nor because of any dissatisfaction with what it had meant in my life. My sixty years were full and fulfilling in so many ways. But the time came when I had to make a very important decision.

Chapter 6

The Painful Decision

A month before the 2017 Baltimore-Washington Annual Conference was to begin, I had no idea how important it was going to be, at least for me personally. Most of the business at an annual conference is predictably routine. For those of us who are retired, there likely wouldn't be much of interest. We'd want to be supportive of the conference and our active colleagues, but we had no particular stake in any outcomes. That was to change. Two or three weeks prior to conference, my attention was called to recent decisions by the church's Judicial Council and our conference's Board of Ordained Ministry. These decisions were to have fateful consequences.

Judicial Council Decisions

The Judicial Council is the church's supreme court, charged with ruling on issues of church law that have been referred to it and dealing with appeals and petitions. On its April 2017 docket, the council had a petition from the South Central Jurisdiction on whether a newly elected Western Jurisdiction bishop, who was in a same-gender marriage, could be allowed to continue as a bishop of the church. The basis of the appeal was a provision in the church's *Book of Discipline* that provides that "self-avowed practicing homosexuals are not to be certified as candidates, ordained as ministers, or appointed to serve in The United Methodist Church." Prior to her election as a bishop, Karen P. Oliveto had been an ordained elder since 1985, serving in a number of pastorates, on the faculty and administrative staff of the Pacific School of Religion, and, most recently, as senior minister of the very large Glide Memorial United Methodist Church in San Francisco. The question before the council was whether she, being in a same-gender marriage, could properly be elected and consecrated as a bishop.

The council first determined that it had jurisdiction in the matter, despite the fact that the South Central Jurisdiction could not, legally, appeal the action by another jurisdiction. The council held that the consecration of a bishop is an action on behalf of the whole church, not simply the electing jurisdiction. That conclusion was disputed by a dissent of two members. The legal technicalities here may be of little interest to most readers; but underlying the technicalities was the council's underscoring and perhaps even expanding the meaning of the church's prohibition of clergy status or appointment of "self-avowed practicing homosexuals."

That point of church law, enacted in 1984, had been reaffirmed by subsequent General Conferences. Nevertheless, its enforcement was uneven. In fact, the church has operated under a kind of "don't ask, don't tell" understanding. Indisputably, there have been homosexual persons in United Methodist ministry, but they have generally remained in the closet. Moreover, previous judicial rulings had specified that the term "self-avowed" meant the person had made a statement to a bishop, district superintendent, or conference board of ordained ministry, and that applying the term "practicing homosexual" required specifying physical acts. In a notable Wisconsin case, a minister who was charged with being a "self-avowed practicing homosexual" because she was in a committed same-gender relationship was persistently asked at a church trial to provide details. She refused and was acquitted of that charge.

In its 2017 decision, however, the Judicial Council held that being in a same-gender marriage constituted "self-avowal" unless it could be proved otherwise. Additionally, it ruled in separate referrals involving two annual conference actions that a board of ordained ministry was obligated to inquire about conformity of candidates to all provisions of church law, including the one about homosexual practice. No more "don't ask, don't tell"!

That point would affect not only candidates for ordained ministry but all those currently in service. At the beginning of the clergy executive session of each annual conference, the district superintendents are expected to certify that all clergy are "blameless" in their practice of ministry. I'm not sure anybody is altogether "blameless," as the official report will generally affirm while indicating that in a few cases clergy are being reviewed and counseled. However, I wonder whether that Judicial Council ruling, if followed scrupulously, would lead to careful investigation of all clergy in respect to sexual orientation. Why is that so? By its ruling that all candidates for ordination could not be "self-avowed practicing homosexuals" and that being in a same-gender union or marriage constituted such a self-avowal, the council was, in effect, calling into question all existing as well as prospective ordained clergy. And if the district superintendents had to certify the blamelessness of all clergy, then that could readily lead to careful exploration of the sexual life and relationships of all clergy. And that could bring an end to a "don't ask, don't tell" policy, not only for prospective ordinands but also for the whole company of clergy.

That concerns me greatly. The relevant provision in the *Book of Discipline* seems clear enough. But it is bad church law. And the church is not just about law, good or bad. Indeed, the *Book of Discipline* itself is not just a law book. It is about larger issues of faith and mission, which, in the end, transcend law. The troubled history of United Methodists grappling with issues of homosexuality shows clearly that the state of the question remains open. I shall say more about this below, but this fact means that rigid enforcement of church law despite strong, principled dissent comes down to legalism. Could there not be greater spiritual elbow room, allowing for a deeper consensus to gather over time instead of forcing the conscience of those in disagreement? Might we United Methodists also note, with respect, how several other mainline Protestant denominations have dealt more gently with this issue?

I was also bothered, perhaps even more, by the Judicial Council's rhetoric. It cited, with obvious approval, the following statement in the *Book of Discipline* (par. 304.3):

> While persons set apart by the Church for ordained ministry are subject to all the frailties of the human condition and the pressures of society, they are required to maintain the highest standards of holy living in the world. The *Social Principles* practice of homosexuality is incompatible with Christian teaching. Therefore self-avowed practicing homosexuals are not to be certified as candidates, ordained as ministers, or appointed to serve in The United Methodist Church.

That provision of the *Discipline* harkens back to one of the Social Principles, adopted in 1972, which found the "practice of homosexuality" to be "incompatible with Christian teaching."

I'll address that point later. But I'm struck by the fact that no General Conference has specified the exact meaning of "incompatible with Christian teaching." And the language of "highest standards of holy living" could be an invitation to self-righteousness among those who have been duly qualified. Does the fact that I have been approved mean that in the judgment of my peers I "maintain the highest standards of holy living in the world"? What does "standards" mean in this context? What does "holy" mean? Might the language of Paul's 1 Corinthians 13 somehow better fit, and even John Wesley's view of the centrality of love? I'll return to this below.

The Presenting Case

Notwithstanding my questions about the Judicial Council's rulings, they would not by themselves have prompted the action I was to take. I know enough of the ebb and flow of church politics to recognize that even bad decisions can be repaired in time. Much of my ministry has involved seeking repairs and reforms, even if I have to acknowledge my own need to change with experience and greater insight.

But the issues posed by the Judicial Council were to take on very specific meaning in my Baltimore-Washington Conference.

At the same time I read those decisions, I learned that T. C. Morrow, whose candidacy for deacon's orders had previously been approved by the conference Board of Ordained Ministry, was now to be held up. While her candidacy was not terminated, she would not be presented to the clergy executive session for provisional approval. The board's decision, set forth in a letter to her and by a statement by the board's chairperson to the executive session, was based on the Judicial Council's decision, which the board wanted to review further. She had been presented to the 2016 clergy executive session, receiving a strong majority of the votes but just a few votes short of the supermajority required. The board indicated it would bring her forward again, in 2017. But now, subsequent to the

Judicial Council's rulings and the board's hasty preconference action, she was not to be presented after all.

There was but one reason for this: Ms. Morrow was in a same-gender marriage. In all other respects she amply fulfilled all requirements and expectations. She was (and is) an effective leader, engaged in service to an anti-torture group that has done much to expose the realities and illegalities of the use of torture. With her spouse, she had cared for foster children, and she had served as a highly respected part-time member of her church staff.

I had first met her when she was at Wesley Theological Seminary, where she was a very strong student. And she had been a part-time staff person with the Churches' Center for Theology and Public Policy, which I served as a board member throughout its history. I had come to know and value her greatly as a person and as a devoted servant of the wider church.

What was to happen? When I learned of the board's decision not to present her I was deeply troubled. Gradually the question came to me, How could I remain in the clergy circle when such a fine person was excluded? Denied progress toward ordination for that one reason alone? What should I do about it?

It comes down to personal relationships.

As I reflected on this over the next few days, it seemed ever more clear that the time for talk alone had ended. I had to act. I discussed the possibility of surrendering my own ordination credentials with Carolyn, with the pastor of the church we attended, with the two leading pastors of T. C. Morrow's Foundry United Methodist Church, with my brother in Oregon, and with a close friend in the California-Nevada Annual Conference who had dealt with these issues for many years. I did not discuss it with T. C. herself, not wanting her to feel any responsibility for my actions. I prepared a statement and had a letter for presentation to our new bishop, along with my ordination certificates.

I had decided that if, as a result of conference debate, T. C.'s name would go forward after all, I would take no action—not even if she lost the supermajority vote (now it had to be three-fourths), provided she received at least a majority of the clergy votes. The board indicated at the outset that it would not bring her name forward. Much debate ensued. The presiding bishop ruled that the board's decision would have to hold.

As the debate proceeded, and the bishop made her ruling, I knew that it was time for me to act. The bishop graciously allowed me to speak to a point of personal privilege. I don't think she knew what I was going to do! I proceeded with my statement:

> Thank you, bishop and colleagues, for this moment of personal privilege. I was ordained an elder almost exactly sixty years ago. My wife, Carolyn, and I celebrated our sixtieth anniversary last summer. We have shared the beauties and joys of ministry throughout those years. I have had many privileges and opportunities to serve the church and its people at all levels.
>
> However, my heart breaks for T. C. Morrow and for others like her with gifts and graces for ordained ministry who have been excluded as a result of bad church law, applied legalistically and hurtfully. I've had to ask myself, how could I remain inside the association of clergy when someone like her must remain outside and even be stigmatized by language of the Judicial Council.
>
> I have concluded that even now, in the twilight years of my life and ministry, I must join with T. C. and others outside the clergy circle by surrendering my credentials today. I do this with a heavy heart, but knowing that Dietrich Bonhoeffer was right about there being a cost of discipleship at every stage in our life as Christians.
>
> Others here may be tempted to follow my example. *I hope not.* I beg all of you to remain within the circle. If you think as I do, let me be your representative, carrying with me your affirmation of those who have been

What about your own privilege and ability to make decision

> excluded and your resolve to seek healing of church law
> and practice. And may the grace of the Lord Jesus Christ
> be with you.

In a cover letter to Bishop LaTrelle Easterling, I said, "Be
assured that this action in no way embodies a criticism of
your work as bishop nor my high esteem for colleagues in
ministry," and noted that I had urged others not to leave
ordained ministry as I had felt compelled to do.

I think the bishop was a bit shocked. As I handed my
credentials to her, up front in the auditorium, she asked if
I would reconsider. No, I replied, I could not. Then, with
tears in her eyes, she called for a moment of prayer, invit-
ing clergy to lay hands on my shoulders, as many did. Then,
after finishing a gracious prayer, which included appreciation for my years of ministry, she called for a conference
break. Many fellow clergy came forward to greet me, as did
the bishop herself. I told her I was sorry to have had to do
this during her very first hour presiding over an annual conference. And then it was over.

I could wish the bishop had ruled otherwise on whether
T. C. Morrow's name could be brought forward. But, in fair-
ness, she had been a bishop for only a few months, and this
was her first experience of presiding over an annual conference. Moreover, her vocational background prior to her own
ordination was as a lawyer, and these were issues of church
law. A bishop has to find some balance between legal supervi-
sion and theological leadership. But whatever my reservations
about her ruling in this instance, I remain grateful for the way
she responded to my action. It was fair, generous, and caring.

T. C. Morrow's own response to the board's disappoint-
ing decision was to show extraordinary grace and dignity,
affirming that she would remain in candidacy status and hope
for change in church policy and action. Her response was yet
another testament of her fitness for ministry, both in terms of
character and in her discernment of larger realities at work.

The Aftermath

My decision to surrender my ordination was truly painful. My journey through all those years serving the church as an ordained minister was traveled with love for The United Methodist Church, for its people, and for its service to Christ—it was a long, formative journey that helped shape the essence of who I am. And I was leaving a circle of collegiality and the role I played in that circle. Nevertheless, I concluded that the issues posed by the Judicial Council and the inability of the conference to proceed with T. C. Morrow's preordination stages left me with no alternative. I could have voiced strong objection, but I have often used the spoken word about these issues. The time had come when an *action*, particularly by somebody with my background and visibility in the church, could speak much louder than words.

It soon became evident that my action did speak loudly. I received many messages of support from around the church, including some from leaders, among them several retired bishops. I was particularly grateful for a statement of support from Bishop Joseph Yeakel. I had much interaction with him when I was chair of the conference Board of Ordained Ministry, and he had enabled my ten years of deeply fulfilling ministry at Foundry Church. I wasn't sure how he, one of the church's preeminent authorities on church law, would react to my decision to leave ordained ministry, but he was altogether supportive.

A prominent seminary dean wrote to say, "Thank you for your sad and courageous act. . . . Your act was a symbolic and strong critique of the UMC's persistent rejection and restrictions on LGBTQ persons, who are precious children of God and whose ministries the church needs now more than ever." She was one of several who referred to my action as "courageous." But, with due appreciation, I can't say that it was. As a retired minister, I had comparatively little to lose. In fact, I can still do most of the things I could do before, both within and beyond the church. Besides, this action really wasn't about me; it was about the good people who have suffered rejection by the church.

Still, the statements of support were welcome. The action had quickly become publicized in church circles around the country, and the messages came from near and far. One prominent Southern California pastor wrote to say, "Thank you for your witness, and for your consistent word and presence through the years. I'm prayerfully hopeful that the [UMC] Commission on a Way Forward will bring a new vision." A retired Arizona pastor noted that I had not made the decision lightly and expressed the hope that I'd continue to seek change. A retired New England pastor questioned whether I should have used the word "surrender" about giving up the clergy credentials: "There ought to be a better word than 'surrender' to describe the action you took on behalf of us all. How about something along the lines of a gift to the church. . . . It was not a retreat in any way." That's true enough. My action certainly was not an abandonment of the ongoing struggle.

More than one hundred of the Baltimore-Washington Conference clergy signed a letter of support. It was also signed by clergy from more than thirty annual conferences from different parts of the country. That statement included the words, "Now is the time to welcome the prayers, gifts, service, and witness of LGBTQI people as members and candidates for ordained ministry in our United Methodist congregations." And, "We lament and decry that United Methodism maintains and enforces exclusionary, discriminatory, and oppressive laws and practices which limit the full participation of LGBTQI people." I hope my action will have helped energize others.

To be sure, there were a few messages from people who strongly disagreed with my views, one or two of whom said, in effect, that they were glad I had "surrendered" my credentials. I don't want to take myself too seriously, and I appreciated the efforts by such critics to help me achieve that objective!

A church administrator of a different denomination invited me to consider ordination in his church. I was grateful for the thought, but as a lifelong Methodist I wasn't about to leave my church.

In the months since my decision, I have had no moments of regret, other than regretting the need to do what I did. But I have also had occasion to organize my thinking about ordination more carefully and to probe a bit more the theological, ethical, and pastoral dimensions of what I had done.

I will further explore those dimensions in the chapters that follow, noting the connections with part 1 of this book.

Chapter 7

Theological Perspective

I explored the theological meaning of ordination in chapter 1. What light does that shed on my action to surrender my ordination credentials? What does it mean to speak of ordination theologically? Recall that I spoke of ordination as a representative ministry. Most directly, an ordained minister is representative of the church—a statement by the church that this minister can, on the whole, be trusted to represent what the church is all about. And since the church seeks to represent Christ, and Christ represents God, ordination is ultimately a statement about how the ordained represents God and the purposes of God. Nobody can do that perfectly, but the ordained minister should strive to do so within the limits of human capabilities.

The Witness of Scripture and Tradition

Chapter 1 did not deal specifically with issues posed by homosexuality; now we must address them directly.

The term "homosexuality" was invented in the nineteenth century, and no equivalent or synonymous term appears in either the Old or New Testament. But same-gender sexual activities are referred to in seven places, each of which appears to condemn such practices. Passages in Leviticus 18 and 20

63

are harshly condemnatory. Leviticus 20:13 is most draconian: "If a man lies with a male as with a woman, both of them have committed an abomination; they shall be put to death; their blood is upon them." Few contemporary Christian critics of all homosexual practice would go that far, but such a view did appear a few years ago when an African country was on the verge of turning homosexuality into a capital offense (before that move was softened in the wake of international outrage). Of a handful of New Testament passages on the issue, Paul's words in Romans 1 are the most theologically based. Speaking of how God gave idolatrous sinners up to "degrading passions," Paul lists examples: "women exchanged natural intercourse for unnatural, and in the same way also the men, giving up natural intercourse with women, were consumed with passion for one another. Men committed shameless acts with men and received in their own persons the due penalty for their error" (1:26–27). The passage goes on to list a variety of other serious crimes and sins. Thus, Paul has here identified homosexual activity with idolatrous turning away from God.

In chapter 1, I pointed to the difficulty of biblical literalism, taking passages as proof texts to justify particular conclusions. Among the difficulties here is that Paul can also be quoted as insisting that "women should be silent in the churches. For they are not permitted to speak, but should be subordinate. . . . If there is anything they desire to know, let them ask their husbands at home" (1 Cor. 14:33–35). Paul even insisted upon proper head covering for women: "Judge for yourselves: is it proper for a woman to pray to God with her head unveiled? Does not nature itself teach you that if a man wears long hair, it is degrading to him, but if a woman has long hair, it is her glory?" (1 Cor. 11:13–14).

Paul has here made factual claims extending beyond basic theology: "Does not nature itself teach you?" Perhaps that is equally true of his statements about what we call homosexuality when he speaks of how women and men "exchanged natural intercourse for unnatural." His comments about idolatry are recognizably theological; his illustrations of such sin necessarily depend upon factual accuracy and not only theological principle.

Similar points can be raised about references to same-gender sexual relationships in church tradition. Writings of early church theologians (the patristics) occasionally make reference to such relationships. For example, in *Confessions* (written about 400 CE), Augustine writes, "Those shameful acts against nature, such as were committed at Sodom, ought everywhere and always to be detested and punished. If all nations were to do such things, they would be held guilty of the same crime by the law of God, which has not made men so that they should use one another in this way" (6.11). A century earlier, Eusebius of Caesarea writes that "having forbidden all unlawful marriage, and all unseemly practice, and the union of women with women and men with men, he [God] adds: do not defile yourselves with any of these things" (*Proof of the Gospel* 4.10). And Basil the Great concludes that "he who is guilty of unseemliness with males will be under discipline for the same crime as adulterers."

This pushes us beyond biblical traditional literalism and proof-texting. Insofar as particular texts are cited to justify conclusions, one must carefully note what is theologically fundamental and what is perceived factually. For instance, Augustine's views on sexuality were all colored by his own promiscuous early years. And one would have to distinguish between his views about sexuality and his much more profound contributions to our understanding of God's grace. Thus we are driven, in our uses of Scripture and tradition, to distinguish those aspects of the writing that are basic to our faith from other aspects that are limited by cultural views and historical conditions. It may well be that some ancient writings exhibit both theological depth and factual wisdom. But a given writing may illustrate one without the other.

In chapter 1 we discussed the centrality of God's love to all theology. I referred there to several theological entry points that may prove helpful as we proceed.

Covenant

As we have seen, the term "covenant" is basic to scriptural theology. It is God's relationship with humanity. The term means agreement, but it is more than that. It is not a "contract" that God and humanity have agreed to. It is God's deep, unbreakable affirmation of humanity and our invitation to respond. There is a sense in which it includes everything else theologically.

The church can be characterized as a covenantal community, one made up of people who understand themselves to be in covenant with God and therefore with one another. This means that the members of a covenantal community are bound together by their understanding of the meaning of a shared faith and by agreements concerning its implications for their lives and mission as a church. What about church law?

A bishop friend of mine used to refer to the United Methodist *Book of Discipline* as our "book of covenant." That is not a bad characterization, as far as it goes—although some clergy sought to correct it by saying that the Bible is really our book of covenant. But is the *Book of Discipline* more fundamentally a law book or a book about the deeper theological bonds we share? If it is simply a law book, then it records legal actions taken by the General Conference as the denomination's ultimate legislative body (and the church's constitution, which reflects more elaborate enactments). So the covenant, in that sense, is determined by majority vote of a General Conference on any issue. Thus, 51 percent of the delegates can determine the meaning of the covenant for the remaining 49 percent, to take an extreme case. By that understanding, all United Methodists—and specifically all United Methodist clergy—are bound, in covenant, to full conformity with General Conference actions.

The principle is similar to contract theories of secular law, exemplified by such thinkers as Thomas Hobbes and John Locke. We may not agree with what has been enacted, but we agree in advance to accept the penalties should we choose to disobey. Typical theories of civil disobedience hold that when we disobey a law out of a conflict of conscience, then we willingly accept the penalties prescribed by law.

I think a good deal of United Methodist discussion of ecclesial disobedience is framed by exactly such secular understandings of contract. That is why both General Conference and the Judicial Council play so pivotal a role in current debates over church law governing homosexuality. Up to a point, such an understanding may be practically helpful and theologically sound.

But the church's covenant really is at a deeper level. Qualifications for ordination include willingness to submit to the order and discipline of the church, but ordination is about much more than order and discipline. It is about being a representative of the church's understanding of its covenant with God and the ties of love and mutual caring among its people. This is more about grace than legalism.

That point is clear in the various statements about faith, theology, and mission in the *Book of Discipline*. We read, for instance, "Grace pervades our understanding of Christian faith and life. By grace we mean the undeserved, unmerited, and loving action of God in human existence through the ever-present Holy Spirit. While the grace of God is undivided, it precedes salvation as 'prevenient grace,' continues in 'justifying grace,' and is brought to fruition in 'sanctifying grace'"; and "We see God's grace and human activity working together in the relationship of faith and good works. God's grace calls forth human response and discipline"; and

We insist that personal salvation always involves Christian mission and service to the world. By joining heart and hand, we assert that personal religion, evangelical witness, and Christian social action are reciprocal and mutually reinforcing.

Scriptural holiness entails more than personal piety; love of God is always linked with love of neighbor, a passion for justice and renewal in the life of the world.

Such statements (many more could be added) are far removed from a spirit of legalism. There is a whole lot of law in this *Book of Discipline*, but the serious covenant view of the church transcends law. It is law in service of covenant, not covenant enabling law.

This bears upon my perception that church law, embodied in the recent judicial rulings and the case of T. C. Morrow, is in deep conflict with the church's essential covenant. But more must be said to make that clear.

Heresy

As I noted before, we don't much like to talk about heresy, bearing in mind certain events in church history involving the burning of heretics at the stake, and so on. But what the term essentially refers to is the boundary separating the church's essential teachings (or dogmas) and beliefs that are in conflict with those essentials. For instance, the rejection of some groups of people as being outside the love of God is heretical among those holding a core belief that God loves everybody. Thus, racism is, in principle, heretical. Theological dualism posits that the forces of goodness, grounded in God, are up against forces of evil with equal power. Many Christians believe in a literal devil, which isn't necessarily that kind of ultimate dualism if the devil is still subordinate to God and will ultimately be defeated by God. There remain difficulties with such a belief, but it is not the same thing as saying that God faces an equal power. It is, however, heretical to assert that God is not ultimately the source and sustainer of all being.

In terms of sexual issues, one could argue that it is heretical to turn sex itself into the essence of being—to worship sex as one's true god. The same would be true of other idolatries, such as materialism and the acquisition of power as the ultimate meaning of life.

To speak of such things as heretical is a reminder that heresy is not all that uncommon and, in fact, that to be human is to struggle against the power of the false gods that separate us from the true God. I shall return to that directly in considering sin.

Creation

I referred in chapter 1 to Karl Barth's insightful discussion of the doctrine of creation, with his formula defining creation as the basis and precondition of the covenant, and covenant as the meaning of creation. That is a striking way to put it, provided we don't think of the whole of creation, the universe, the natural world, and so on, only in instrumental terms. We remember the words of Genesis 1: "God saw that it was good." There is a whole lot of mystery there. We continue to learn more and more about the intricate, interlocking aspects of creation, from the most intimate forms of life to the vast, sweeping reaches of the unfathomable universe.

For our purposes, in dealing with issues of sexuality, the question is how this important physical aspect of creation relates to grace and covenant. Does creation disclose its own meaning, apart from loving relationship with God and fellow humanity? When people attempt to justify absolute rejections of all homosexual "practice" by appeal to isolated scriptural texts and passages taken from patristic writings, they soon discover that there are problems—at least the problem of statements from the same sources that most people today would reject out of hand. It is not unusual when confronting the difficulties of sexual practices for people to revert to some form of natural law. That means taking a view that it is the "nature" of some activities to be moral or immoral, on the face of it. In the Christian natural law tradition, based ultimately on Aristotelian thought via Thomas Aquinas, everything has an "end" (*telos*), a defining goal or purpose. Sex, for instance, can be seen as having the defining purpose of procreation; that is what is was created for. On the basis of this supposed purpose, an early-twentieth-century pope declared contraception "intrinsically evil."

The question is whether creation, apart from covenant and grace, sufficiently discloses its own ends.

Sin

That issue is joined when we approach the question of sin. Seen as separation from God, as we spoke of it in chapter 1, sin has to take on a greater theological meaning than the simple violation of particular commandments or functions of natural law. I will examine whether homosexual practice is necessarily sinful in the next chapter. But here I must record why my church's actions, by Judicial Council and the conference Board of Ordained Ministry, led to my action.

It is not a question of whether sexual attitudes and actions can be sinful; surely they can be. Much of the UM Social Principles analysis of sexual immorality is both clear and persuasive. Any form of sexual exploitation, whether by heterosexual or homosexual persons, must be rejected. There is, I believe, a very strong consensus among United Methodists about that. The issue is not even whether other United

Methodists can, in good faith, disagree with my views and those who share them. Votes in General Conferences reveal a divided church, with approximately 60 percent supporting the current positions on homosexuality and approximately 40 percent opposed. Such a division has persisted for many years, and I suppose it largely reflects the thinking of United Methodists—noting that there are significant regional and national differences of viewpoint.

The problem is that the rulings in question have absolutized views that, at this stage in the church's life, are relative. The state of the question, currently, is that there are deep differences among people of good faith. In the final chapter I will seek to address this political situation in the church. But here I want to observe that when relative questions are treated as absolutes, we risk idolatry. We make a "god" out of our insufficiently examined views. In that sense, all of us do, from time to time, hold strong views and commitments that should not be treated as absolutes. Most of us have changed our minds about things, abandoning or modifying views we've been pretty sure about. This means that even strongly held convictions should be accompanied by a degree of intellectual humility—saying to ourselves, in effect, that we are open to new insight, new leadings by the Spirit. God is the only absolute, and none of us know everything about God!

We have to make judgments about what is sinful or what is not sinful, but in identifying anything as sin we have to be very careful. In chapter 1, I spoke of sin as "any attitudes, acts, or practices that stand in the way of receiving the grace of God." God's grace is, we believe, unconditional. We don't have to earn it, we don't deserve it. But we can, and often do, create barriers to receiving it. Those barriers are the essence of sin. Again, judgments about what interferes with receiving God's grace must be very well founded. If we're wrong about this we may, ironically, have ourselves impeded the full working of God's grace.

We often think of sin primarily in individual terms. All of us, individually, are capable of sin—maybe even prone to sin. But isn't sin also a collective fact? Can't we engage in sin together? Can't our institutions embody sin? That is, can't our institutions create barriers to people receiving God's grace? Isn't it even true that the church can, through doctrine, actions, policies, and laws, create barriers to receiving the free gift of God's grace? On the whole, I believe the church embodies God's grace. But not always.

I am old enough to remember when the Methodist Church (and most other American churches) had policies supporting racial segregation. When I was a college student I worked for a couple of years part-time in a small church in Stockton, California, that was identified at the time as one of only one hundred Methodist churches *in the whole country* that was racially integrated. During that era, venturesome African Americans were sometimes turned away at the doors of white churches. The Methodist Central Jurisdiction was a structure of racial segregation. Was that not a barrier to the church's full reception of God's grace?

By its action, the Judicial Council has judged homosexual practice as necessarily a form of sin. In doing so, it has reinforced the view that homosexual practice as a sin is integral to the essential teachings of the United Methodist Church. The Judicial Council's ruling was not simply rhetorical, restating with approval the idea that homosexual practice is necessarily incompatible with Christian teaching. It did not explore in any way the theological rationale for that view, as that might relate to other, deeper UM teaching about Christian faith. The council's action absolutized that position by making it negatively determinative in the selection of ordained ministers—those who would represent the essential nature of the church. Was this action one that created barriers to God's grace? Was it, in that sense, an expression of the collective sin of the church? We should ponder that question, both practically and theologically.

For me, there remained the question: How could I, as an ordained minister of this church, represent the church at this very important point?

I could, of course, remain an ordained United Methodist minister, continuing to voice my strong disapproval of the church's position on the issues at hand. I have been doing that for many years since first elected as a General Conference delegate in 1988. That is what I urged like-minded fellow UM clergy to do when I begged them not to follow my example by surrendering their credentials. But for my part, words were no longer enough. I now had to act in such a way that my words would have to be taken more seriously—that this was not simply an intellectual position, arrived at by one of the church's teachers of ethics, but a part of my own faith commitment.

Christian Freedom

Paul's view of the freedom we have in our faith in Christ is largely represented in his Letter to the Galatians. Essentially, it means that we no longer are bound by legalism. We do not, indeed we cannot, earn our salvation by works of the law. Paul's view can easily be misunderstood. Indeed, it probably was misunderstood by the New Testament Letter of James, where we read that "faith apart from works is barren" (2:20). Paul, of course, had insisted that what we do matters. But through our faith in God's grace we no longer have to act out of fear but rather in loving response to God's immeasurable gift.

We are haunted by our moral failures, but not because God will no longer love and forgive us. Our moral failures are largely their own punishment, because they take us away from the truly abundant life and because they so often break the fabric of human community that is so important in that life. An ordained minister cannot be perfect—despite the odd question UM candidates have to answer about expecting to be made perfect in this life. But much depends upon whether we seek to be more loving and more intelligent in facing the dilemmas of moral decision making.

A necessary part of God's gift of grace is free will. Much of life is determined, of course, by circumstances we have inherited and by other things that are beyond our control. We do not have perfect freedom, but neither are our actions totally determined. Paul Tillich was right in treating this as a "polarity," the juxtaposition of "freedom and destiny." By "destiny" he meant all that makes us who we are and that shapes our actions, sometimes completely beyond our control. By "freedom" he meant our capacity to interact with those forces of destiny, helping to determine what they will become and thereby creating new forms of destiny for the future. Freedom and destiny. We are not totally free, but neither are we completely determined.

Consider the homosexuality issue through that lens. Some people, mostly those who are most judgmental about this, argue that homosexual identity and practice are simply chosen. People decide to be homosexual and to act it out. Others disagree, treating homosexuality as a biological, perhaps genetic, given. I will explore this issue further in the next chapter. But suppose Tillich's polarity is right. Even if homosexual identity is not entirely a totally natural inheritance (a destiny), and instead we have a strong inclination in that direction—does it really matter that we live out our lives on the basis of that inclination?

It is safe to say that most people are not born with or acquire such an inclination; but, clearly, some do. Why does this matter? Are there sound ethical reasons why a person with homosexual inclinations should remain celibate? We must also look at that in the ethics chapter to follow.

It is not enough to cite a few passages of Scripture or snippets of writing by some past Christian theologians or views of "natural law." What is at stake, finally, is whether homosexual practice is invariably sinful. Does it necessarily constitute a chosen set of attitudes and behaviors that create barriers to receiving God's unconditional loving grace? If so, should it constitute adequate grounds for excluding someone from ordained ministry? And would it mean that the Judicial Council was right and that a T. C. Morrow should not be presented for reception into ordained ministry? I plainly do not think so. But let's consider some of these issues further.

Chapter 8

Ethical Implications

*G*iving up my ordination had many ethical implications. As a longtime student and professor of Christian social ethics, I've had to consider my actions carefully through the ethical lens. That should be evident in the preceding chapters. Now I wish to address some of the issues more directly. I've noted already that neither values nor facts can be disregarded. Ethics invariably involves choices in the factual world, although facts alone do not determine the nature and source of our basic values. In this chapter I pursue some of the important factual questions raised by homosexuality before proceeding further with the ethical implications of my decision to leave ordained ministry.

Factual Causes of Sexual Orientation

As a first-time General Conference delegate in 1988, I had to face issues related to homosexuality more directly than ever before. Prior to the conference I received a lot of letters from people seeking to influence my actions and decisions—many, I noted, from Texas, urging me to help the church hold the line on current conservative positions. I had already moved beyond those positions in my thinking, but I still had questions. The time was ripe for the church to establish a study commission on homosexuality with sufficient resources to find the best scientific, theological, and ethical insights available. I authored the legislation adopted by the 1988 General Conference to establish such a task force. It was adopted, and I was appointed to be one of its members.

I had hoped the committee's studies and consultations could lead to closure on the big issues, especially the scientific ones. That wasn't to be. While there had been scientific studies, there seemed to be no clear evidence of what causes people to be heterosexual or homosexual. At that time genetic studies weren't far enough advanced. The social sciences helped a bit through their studies of the self-understanding of gay and lesbian persons, along with studies of social and cultural influences at work. In its final report, the committee developed a list of things that the church could and could not responsibly teach on the subject, such as these:

- The specific causes of homosexual orientation remain unclear, although various scientific theories contribute to our overall understanding.
- The church cannot teach that gay and lesbian persons are generally dysfunctional or characteristically preoccupied with sex—some are and some are not, just like their heterosexual counterparts.
- The church cannot teach that gay and lesbian persons are prone to seduce or corrupt others—some are and some are not, again, just like their heterosexual counterparts.
- The church cannot teach that the same percentage of every society is gay or lesbian. That is not borne out in the limited reputable cross-cultural studies. It does appear that homosexual relations exist in some form in all cultures studied.
- The church cannot teach that sexual orientation is fixed at birth, nor can it teach that it is fixed only after birth. The scientific evidence is insufficient to allow a judgment either way, particularly considering the diverse types of both heterosexuality and homosexuality.

- The church cannot teach that sexual orientation, either heterosexual or homosexual, is deliberately chosen. It is clear that substantial numbers of persons have experienced their sexual orientation from early childhood.
- The church cannot teach that there is a single theory of homosexual orientation or behavior—or, for that matter, of heterosexual orientation or behavior. No one theory is sufficiently supported by empirical evidence to be taught as generally accepted truth.

While these points, summarizing the committee's studies and consultations, were written in 1992, they remain fairly accurate today. Scientific studies conducted in more recent years have not produced any generally accepted single theory accounting for the differences of sexual orientation. Studies have examined identical twins, brain structure in deceased homosexual and heterosexual persons, prenatal hormonal factors, evolutionary issues, and even rams that have homosexual tendencies. It is important to understand that while studies often show differences between persons of different sexual orientation, those differences are not characteristic of *all* subjects examined.

Perhaps the one thing most clear in more recent studies is that there will not prove to be any single causal factor, although there remain significant evidences of some physiological differences accompanying differences of sexual orientation. Mysteriously, for example, gay and lesbian persons are discernibly more likely to be left-handed. That, of course, does not mean that left-handed persons are more likely to be gay or lesbian! Perhaps further study will bring greater clarity, but we cannot expect any single physical factor to close the ongoing debate over causation.

The United Methodist committee observed that in the debate over causation, due credence must be given both to nature and to nurture, if "nurture" refers to all relational and environmental factors that contribute to what we are to become and "nature" means physiological factors that are not environmental or relational.

Perhaps the American Psychological Association got it right when it observed that sexual orientation derives from the complex mixture and interaction of biological and environmental factors. The APA at one time listed homosexuality as a psychological disorder, but it no longer does.

The Ineffectiveness of Conversion Therapy

Can homosexual orientation be changed by therapeutic and other kinds of intervention? Perhaps behavior can be. People can be influenced or even led to change their behaviors. Positive and negative incentives affect behavior. But outward behavior does not necessarily reflect inner feelings and attitudes.

Efforts to intervene and change homosexual orientation may work in some cases, though when that occurs it may simply mean that the orientation is not very deeply rooted. More often, the interventions do more harm than good and are, at best, ineffective. In conversations with gay and lesbian people, I have often been told that they had spent long periods of time trying to change, without success. One therapist who was personally opposed to any homosexual practice, on ethical grounds, reported to the UM committee that he had sought to bring about change in a number of gay and lesbian people, but that he had been successful in only half the cases.

Perhaps the views of psychology professionals are even more impressive. For instance, the American Academy of Child and Adolescent Psychiatry stated in 2012, "Clinicians should be aware that there is no evidence that sexual orientation can be altered through therapy, and that attempts to do so may be harmful. . . . There is no empirical evidence that adult homosexuality can be prevented if gender nonconforming children are influenced to be more gender conforming." The organization added that "such efforts may encourage family rejection and undermine self-esteem, connectedness, and caring, which are important protective factors against suicidal ideation and attempts." Such views are also expressed by the American Academy of Pediatrics, the American Association for Marriage and Family Therapy, the American College of Physicians, the American Counseling Association, the American Medical Association, the American Psychiatric Association, the American Psychoanalytic Association, the American Psychological Association, the American School Counselor Association, the American School Health Association, and the National Association of Social Workers.

The views of such professionals have to be taken seriously. I am particularly dismayed by the psychological, indeed the spiritual, harm that can be done to gay and lesbian people by attempting conversion therapies.

Ethical Consequences

That, in brief, is the factual situation. What ethical conclusions should we draw from this?

Among those who consider homosexual practice to be sinful, there are some who acknowledge that sexual orientation is not simply chosen, but that it must still be considered pathological. The analogy is with birth defects or diseases that are not chosen but still damaging. Nobody chooses to be born with a cleft palate or a brain defect, but insofar as it is possible, therapeutic interventions must be undertaken.

Is that a sound analogy? It finally comes down to whether there is anything "wrong" with homosexual orientation and behaviors.

The United Methodist Social Principles, as we have seen, treat homosexual practice as incompatible with Christian teaching. The question of *why* this is so has continued to dangle over the church since the language was adopted in 1972. We have seen that it is problematical to base such a conclusion on either biblical proof texts or natural law. Standing as it does, the view really comes down to our understanding of sin. Is homosexual practice a sin? Isn't that what is meant by Christians when they identify it as contrary to the teachings of their faith?

I hold the view that, at root, sin is anything in our attitudes or actions that is a barrier to experiencing the freely given grace of God. Is there anything about homosexual orientation or actions that *inevitably* and *necessarily* constitutes such a barrier? I underscore the words "inevitably" and "necessarily" because the language of that Social Principle does not allow any exceptions; nor, consequently, do the exclusion of "self-avowed practicing homosexuals" from ordination and the requirement that ministers must not celebrate the unions of gay and lesbian couples. Those translations of Social Principle into church law are equally absolute, admitting to no exceptions. So the question remains, Why? Can an account be given that passes rigorous ethical muster?

To be sure, some ways of "practicing" homosexuality can be called into ethical question. For example, the sexual abuse of boys and girls by some clergy is manifestly and seriously beyond the pale. So too, obviously, is homosexual rape. That is equally true of heterosexual abuses. Sexual promiscuity, whether homosexual or heterosexual, is also ethically questionable. The United Methodist Social Principle on sexuality is clear about such things. Can these actions be labeled "sin," seen as a barrier to experiencing God's grace? Yes, because such behaviors tend to treat other persons as objects of gratification, not as persons to be respected in their full humanity.

But is it factually true that all, or even many, gay and lesbian people are engaged in such sin?

The United Methodist Committee to Study Homosexuality was, as I said before, disappointed in not finding clear, open-and-shut, scientific evidences at the level of causation. But it did discover one fact of even greater importance. It encountered very strong evidence of the presence in UM churches of homosexual persons who exhibit the gifts and graces and moral disciplines of Christian life at least equal to heterosexual United Methodists. In other words, while seeking factual expertise from physical and social scientists, we had, right before our eyes, even more significant facts within our own churches. How could we ignore that? How could any responsible person fail to weigh that on the ethical scales?

Far from being exploitative, many gay and lesbian Christians have shown extraordinary compassion and care of others. I recall a gay member who, disregarding any personal risk, devoted long hours to the care of a gay man with AIDS when an AIDS diagnosis was a virtual death sentence and it remained unclear whether there was any risk in being exposed to an AIDS patient. Another gay man worked year after year in organizing conferences for caregivers. But typically, gay and lesbian church members were, unless you already knew, indistinguishable from everyone else.

An illustration of that leaps to mind. Several years ago the California-Nevada Annual Conference was engaged in debate over whether it should become a "reconciling" conference. The term refers to a UM local church or conference that openly supports gay and lesbian people and seeks changes in church law. One of the reasons why that conference embraced the "reconciling" level was that Bob Cary, the longtime youth director for the conference, was gay. A large number of clergy in the conference had been influenced deeply by him, including many who had felt the call toward ministry through his counsel. Through his many years of service to the youth of the conference, there had been no hint of scandal of any kind. He was obviously a good person and an unusually effective youth leader. That fact made it impossible for members of the conference to accept stereotypes about gay and lesbian people. Such has often been the case with churches whose members have found gay and lesbian fellow members to be fine persons.

The Question of Same-Gender Marriage

The Judicial Council decision of 2017 specified that a same-sex marriage constituted prima facie evidence of its partners being "self-avowed" practicing homosexuals. Its grounds for that statement were that physical sexual acts have long been considered intrinsic to marriage. Not surprisingly, same-gender marriage has emerged as a key issue in the debates over church teaching and law about homosexuality. It was a central feature in the ordination dispute over T. C. Morrow that led, in large measure, to my action.

There is more than a little irony in this. Negative attitudes toward homosexuality have often equated it with sexual exploitation and promiscuity. But faithful marriage would seem to be exactly the opposite. Let's suppose you do consider homosexual practice to be a sin. In the bonds of marriage, wouldn't it be a lesser form of sin, if sin at all? Why, even if you regard this as sin, would you treat this as such an absolute?

Sometimes it is argued that biblical references to marriage refer to a man and a woman. That is particularly true of the New Testament, and there is no scriptural evidence of this being treated in contrast to any same-gender form of marriage. Moreover, when people call for the scriptural model of marriage they conveniently forget the polygamy that was characteristic of greatly revered figures like Abraham, Isaac, and Jacob, not to mention kings David and Solomon. David's sexual ethic is condemned not for his polygamy but for his awful episode with Bathsheba and his treatment of her husband.

So what is the problem with same-gender marriage? I suppose it is rejected out of hand by people who think it would lead to general acceptance of homosexuality. Of course, any on the other side may emphasize same-gender marriage for the same reason. But there are lots of gay and lesbian couples who want to have the moral dignity of their union to be seen and appreciated by society. Many had been living together before the Supreme Court legalized such marriages nationally in 2015. Writing for a majority of the court, Justice Anthony Kennedy offered this eloquent statement:

> No union is more profound than marriage, for it embodies the highest ideals of love, fidelity, devotion, sacrifice, and family. In forming a marital union, two people become something greater than once they were. As some of the petitioners in these cases demonstrate, marriage embodies a love that may endure even past death. It would misunderstand these men and women to say they disrespect the idea of marriage. Their plea is that they do respect it, respect it so deeply that they seek to find its fulfillment for themselves. Their hope is not to be condemned to live in loneliness, excluded from one of civilization's oldest institutions. They ask for equal dignity in the eyes of the law. The Constitution grants them that right.

Could any church pronouncement or writing by an ethicist have put it better? There also are practical legal issues here, including rights to make health care decisions, survivorship, and tax advantages. But the heart of the matter is set forth by Justice Kennedy. The court did not require any clergy to officiate at same-gender weddings. Indeed, no clergyperson is legally required to perform *any* wedding. But the court placed civil law in a morally more defensible position on this issue than that of The United Methodist Church.

Why have I referred to such marriages as "same-gender" rather than "same-sex"? The two terms often are used as synonyms. However, the word "sex" carries more of a physical connotation than the word "gender." The physical aspect may be and usually is involved. But marriage, while usually involving physical sexual intimacies, is about much more. It is a commitment of loving relationship. As the typical wedding vow puts it, "to have and to hold from this day forward, for better, for worse, for richer, for poorer, in sickness and in health, to love and to cherish until we are parted by death." Such a commitment of mutual caring embodies love that is much more than physical sex and more than ephemeral sentimentality. In regrettable cases, it may prove necessary to dissolve a marriage. But in principle, and more often than not in practice, this is a serious, lifetime commitment.

The fact that T. C. Morrow was in a same-gender marriage was of the essence of her being held up as a candidate for ordination, and therefore very important to my own decision. How could the church dismiss the moral dignity of her marriage in rejecting her progress toward ordination?

Dealing with Doubts and Dilemmas in Ethics

Not all cases are as clear as this one. Sometimes serious ethical decision making forces us to decide when we can't be so sure. In point of fact, we probably cannot be absolutely sure about very much in this life! I was intrigued to note that the Judicial Council provided a hint of uncertainty—the barest hint—in its ruling that same-gender marriage is prima facie evidence of a self-avowal of the practice of homosexuality. The council held that such a conclusion is "rebuttable" with sufficient evidence to the contrary. That means that the fact of such a marriage equates to a couple's public declaration of their engagement in physical sexual activity unless it can be proven otherwise. How could it be proven? Perhaps issues related to injury, illness, or age could arise to preclude such activity. Then the burden of proof might be met.

The use of legal presumption and placing the burden of proof would be familiar to any student of law. And that is often a good way to deal with doubts and dilemmas in ethics. However, I think the council got it almost exactly wrong. In ethical terms, the presumption should be on the other side. If a candidate for ordination is in a same-gender marriage, then the presumption should be that, in fulfillment of those wedding vows, the couple are not engaged in promiscuous or exploitative sexual activity. I state that as an ethical observation, not as a legal conclusion. Insofar as church law has been correctly stated by the council, in this instance it has not sufficiently taken into account the weight of church theology and the deeper commitments of ordination.

A further note can be added, in assessing the ethical issues. Even those who consider same-gender sexual relationships always to be sinful need to decide how serious this sin is in comparison with other sins. The point emerged, a bit humorously, in one of the hearings conducted by the UM Committee to Study Homosexuality. An older pastor testified before the committee that he had sought to change a few homosexual persons and that he regarded their actions as a sin. He was asked, if this truly is a sin, whether the church should be singling it out as it has. "Oh, probably not," he replied. Church law certainly has singled homosexuality out for special emphasis. Should it?

Years ago, similar attention was given to divorce. Clergy were admonished not to remarry any divorced persons unless it could be shown that they were not the guilty party. Today the church's attitude and law have changed, almost abruptly. Divorce is still viewed negatively, but there are no absolute condemnations in church law. In fact, there are ordained clergy who have been divorced, either before or after ordination. Divorce is viewed with sadness and regret, but not with punitive legislation.

In weighing the relative seriousness of what some consider to be sin, an important consideration is always who is being hurt, and how much. Who are the victims, if any? Convincing answers can be given in clear cases of sexual abuse and depersonalization. But when homosexual persons are living responsibly, it is hard to see that anybody is being hurt, really. The question of how homosexual persons themselves are being hurt is one I shall address in the next chapter, on the pastoral imperatives we face.

Other Forms of Sexual Life

First, however, I want to comment on something that might have occurred to many readers of this chapter. Why have I limited most of this discussion to gay and lesbian people? Why not speak of bisexual and transgender people and others alluded to by the alphabetic LGBTQI abbreviation? I'm not sure I fully understand the *Q* and the *I* and how they might impact this chapter on ethics. So far as the *B* is concerned, if it means bisexual, then it is a reference to people whose orientation is both homosexual and heterosexual. Church law does not deal with bisexuality, as such, but only with the part that is homosexual in character. But what about those who practice their sexuality in both directions? I have done little study of what bisexuality might mean in practice, and it is in no way involved in the basic issues I'm addressing in this book.

The *T*, or transgender, question isn't involved here, either. But I must note that it does not appear in church law. There are no prohibitions of transgender persons being ordained nor of weddings involving transgender persons. Everything, in such cases, must depend upon what is the gender of the person being considered, not how that gender was arrived at. I have known a small number of transgender persons in ministry, and my own judgment is that they have arrived at greater wholeness, and effectiveness, as a result of the transition. But again, this has not become a subject for church law and teaching. The subject does illustrate the great complexity of human sexuality and why the church needs to be more careful in its pronouncements and laws.

Conclusion

The ethical considerations I have highlighted in this chapter help to illuminate the basis of my decision to leave ordained ministry. How could I, through my ordination, be viewed as representing a church with such formalized, ill-considered teaching and what I have considered to be bad church law, applied painfully? But even deeper reasons appear in the following chapter.

Chapter 9

A Pastoral Imperative

*B*oth the theological and ethical meanings of ordination played a role in my decision to leave the ordained ministry. But the pastoral meaning of ordination may have been even more important. Why is that so? Oddly, I felt that I could better fulfill the pastoral meaning of ordination by leaving than by remaining ordained.

To be a pastor is to reach out and help people find fulfillment in their life journey—to come to realize the fullness of God's grace, to deal with hardships and sorrows, to be at one with fellow humanity, to be able to celebrate the joys of life. And much more. To be a pastor is to experience the depth of the goodness of God, even if it is through a sharing of the pain that is common to us all. I had many pastoral experiences even before and after being invited to serve a local church. In fact, one does not have to be ordained to be a pastoral minister, although when one is ordained the church declares that this is someone to whom others can turn with confidence that they will receive that kind of care.

So what was the pastoral basis of my decision?

Responding to Hurt Inflicted by the Church

Gay and lesbian people have been stigmatized, en bloc, by the church, seemingly without exception, if they are in any way engaging in sexual activity. I know no other way to interpret that sweeping statement in the Social Principles other than that it judges homosexuality, when expressed physically, to be contrary to Christian teaching. If contrary to the gospel, to Christian teaching, then it is sin, pure and simple. Which means that gay and lesbian people, by engaging in physical expressions of their sexual orientation, are living in sin. That includes even same-gender marriage as a lifelong covenant of faithfulness. The point was underscored by the Judicial Council's citing of language in the *Book of Discipline* that limits ordained ministry to persons with the highest standards of holy living. Gay and lesbian persons are treated specifically as not living by those standards.

We have to notice that elements of ambiguity accompanying such teaching were not referred to in the council's decision. For example, the Social Principles include this statement: "We implore families and churches not to reject or condemn lesbian and gay members and friends" (par. 161-G). "Implore" is a very strong verb! But how could a gay or lesbian person not feel that they have been rejected? I do not think many gay and lesbian persons have been rejected for church membership, even if their sexual orientation is known, although there have been some cases. More often, a local church's rejection is expressed as avoidance, with gay and lesbian persons not feeling welcomed and not being accepted as normal participants in the life of the church, including positions of leadership. The words directed to churches as well as families that they should not reject such persons were not adopted in a vacuum. Rather, they were framed in response to realities. Aren't such realities a reflection of the words about incompatibility with Christian teaching?

In respect to same-gender marriages, has the language of the *Discipline*, underscored by the Judicial Council, not said in effect that the spouses are living in sin? Couldn't one argue, with the U.S. Supreme Court, that such marriages are commendable relationships that can be deeply fulfilling? How can the rejection of those relationships not be deeply hurtful to those who want and need pastoral affirmation from their church?

Some Illustrations

In recent years I have had occasion to talk with people who have felt rejected by the church. One striking example is a woman who was attracted to Foundry Church after it had become a reconciling congregation. She was, before her untimely death from a brain aneurysm, a nationally prominent figure in a leading American professional association. Leading an adult study in the church one day, she remarked that for more than twenty years she had been unable to relate to a church without feeling ostracized. Now, at Foundry, she felt fully accepted. I've no doubt that she was accepted at Foundry, as were many others, and we all grieved over her death. And I have no doubt that she had felt alienated from churches, although Foundry is certainly not the only church where she might have experienced real welcome. But that was her experience.

When the District of Columbia legalized same-gender marriage in 2010, the Dumbarton United Methodist Church in DC announced its willingness to conduct such marriages. In the months preceding the DC action, some of the clergy associated with Dumbarton made plans. These clergy included several who were retired or serving in church-related agencies of one kind or another. It was agreed that such weddings would follow the same guidelines as heterosexual ceremonies, including adequate premarital counseling. Also, two clergy would always conduct such services together.

The first such wedding occurred in March of that year. The two men had been living together for more than twenty years in a de facto covenantal relationship. Years before, one of the two had been a seminary student heading toward ministry, but he had felt rejected by the church. So they were, in effect, alienated from churches throughout their long relationship. After the wedding, however, the couple became very active participants in the life of Dumbarton Church. The pastoral support they had received from the church was exactly the opposite of what they had previously experienced.

A same-gender couple from another state approached Dumbarton in 2011 to be married there. They were active in a church where they were known to be living together. That was not a particular problem, but at the time, marriage could have caused serious problems, including possible rejection and even the loss of employment in their community. At the time, marriage wasn't a legal option in their state, and they felt it would be safer for them if their marriage was not known.

A couple who had been married in California sought to have a religious ceremony in New York State for family members and friends who couldn't be present in California. This reenactment conducted by an ordained minister occurred in a beautiful outdoor setting, not within a church building. Like other weddings, it was preceded by premarital consultation. The really interesting thing about this marriage is that the couple had two children, both borne by one of the women through in vitro fertilization. By the time of the marriage service, both of the boys were teenagers. Both were obviously well-adjusted, quite normal, on their way to manhood. One of the two was able to be at the New York ceremony so he could also experience firsthand a religious recognition of the moral dignity of the marriage of his parents.

What would the General Conference or Judicial Council say about such a case? How would the church address the sons of this marriage? Should they be told that their same-gender parents are living in sin? How might the boys have experienced church school and United Methodist Youth Fellowship? Would they need to hide their parents' same-gender marriage? Could their parents attend those events, in church or school events where parents normally accompany their children? What is a pastor's pastoral responsibility here?

If anything, the children of same-gender spouses are an even more compelling pastoral responsibility of an ordained minister than the parents themselves.

My point is, *these are not hypothetical situations!* These are actual human beings, beloved of God, a part of the God-intended human community of justice and loving-kindness.

These and other pastoral cases came readily to mind when I contemplated the move I was to make at the annual conference on May 31, 2017. Didn't my pastoral responsibility for these people come before everything else? I, of course, could not be pastor in any direct sense to the large number of people who have been stigmatized by official church action. But that church policy was in itself a pastoral action, to be received as such by those who felt rejected. Here was a prominent United Methodist ordained minister, in good standing, who was seeking to be God's pastoral grace to those who have been outside the circle. In a certain sense, I was fulfilling the pastoral meaning of ordination better by leaving my ordination.

Ecclesial Disobedience
to Fulfill Pastoral Responsibility

My action of surrendering clergy credentials was not, in any sense, against church law. Some, who oppose my under-standing of the pastoral responsibility, doubtless welcomed my action. Better for me to be out of the way. Obviously, I haven't seen this in exactly that light. My action was intended to be a clear statement of the wrongness of a bad church law that was being enforced legalistically and hurtfully.

That said, I must acknowledge that there are times when pastoral responsibility must preempt church law among those who are serious about the pastoral dimension of ordained ministry. When that choice seems necessary, it must be made in full recognition of the importance of church law and with a desire to avoid disobedience where morally possible. But such occasions can occur. As noted above, even John Wes-ley confronted the problem when told by Bishop Butler that he should not preach in the Bristol Diocese. Wesley valued his priesthood and provided reasons for his actions. But he and the bishop disagreed, and the bishop had full authority over the diocese in which Wesley continued to preach.

In The United Methodist Church, it is, formally at least, an act of ecclesial disobedience for an ordained minister to conduct a same-gender wedding ceremony. I must make a full disclosure here: Along with other clergy, I have co-officiated in such weddings—always, to be sure, in accordance with every other aspect of regular church practice. Each of the instances described above was a wedding I conducted in this way, although the reenactment ceremony was not done with a fellow clergyperson. (That one instance may not even have been a formal disobedience of church law, since the couple already had been legally married.)

I have not officiated at same-gender weddings in total disregard of church law. I considered those actions to be exceptions, not undertaken lightly. Nor have I been secretive about it, letting it be known through public statements why I have felt it pastorally necessary. In fact, at the beginning I rather expected to be charged with a violation of church law. But neither I nor others in this conference (and a number of other conferences) have experienced any censure—although in other areas there have been charges and even church trials.

But consider: Most of the couples at whose weddings I and others have officiated had been living together faithfully for years. Most had previously felt alienated by church law and the subtle but real forces of ostracism. Don't we *have* to render pastoral service in such situations? Must we not seek to be channels of God's grace?

Pastoral Responsibility for Those Who Disagree

It may occur to more than one reader that while ordained ministers have a pastoral responsibility to those who have been stigmatized, we also are pastors to those who object to our support of such persons. True enough. During my pastorate at Foundry Church, and while it was becoming a reconciling congregation, it seemed clear to me that we had an immediate responsibility to those who disagreed with that action. During the Sunday services following the administrative board's action, I spoke to the congregation about this. To be truly "reconciling" meant we could not reject people who disagreed with that action. As it turned out, not very many seriously objected. Most of those who did had only been afraid of the consequences of the action for church membership. In fact, Foundry lost very few members and gained many more. Even those who disagreed on the basis of theological or ethical principle did not, on the whole, consider this to be all that important an issue. But there are people who are opposed to change in church law because they consider those church laws to be a bulwark against the acceptance of sin. How are we to minister, pastorally, to these people while attending to those who have been injured through stigma and rejection?

I do not consider these to be equivalent subjects of pastoral need. On the one hand, those who are being injured; on the other hand, those who wish to maintain restrictions that are causing the injury. Nevertheless, even that second group is made up of people who need pastoral guidance. I recall that for a long time in my own case I had considered homosexuality to be either a sin or a pathology or some mixture of the two. As an ethicist I didn't regard this as among the greatest moral problems facing humanity, but that is where I was.

What changed my views more than anything else, as I've already noted above, was my contact with gay and lesbian persons who clearly evidenced the gifts and graces of Christian life. This leads me to suppose that one of the best kinds of pastoral guidance here can be to draw more people into relationships. That is parallel to studies of racism in the early 1940s that showed how interracial contact of equals could be especially helpful, if participants are truly equal. So the normalization of participation in church life by gay and lesbian persons can help immensely with their acceptance. I might note that the views of many people have been changed by discovery that their own children or grandchildren, or others close to them, are gay or lesbian. It hasn't always worked that way, but often it has.

There are also those who have inherited instinctive homophobia, irrational feelings of aversion in the presence of known gay or lesbian persons. I am not a psychologist and have no real insight into how to minister to more severe forms of homophobia. But, again, I suspect that fostering normal relationships may be the best "cure." This can help people discover there aren't reasons to be so fearful. I do find it striking that such attitudes are more likely to be found among men than women. That leads to the suspicion that homophobia is sometimes a reaction to perceived threats to one's dominant masculine role.

Insofar as the negative attitudes are an expression of inherited cultural factors, we can expect change to occur. There is already considerable evidence of change in the United States, where the Supreme Court decision has reinforced parallel changes in public attitudes. That decision, according to a 2017 Gallup poll and Pew Research, appears to be supported by 60 percent of the population. But there are regional variations, and The United Methodist Church may be strongest, numerically, in regions with more negative cultural attitudes toward homosexuality.

Change is occurring. But in the meantime people are still being hurt. And that is at the heart of my action to surrender ordination as a pastoral support for people whom the church's law is hurting.

Chapter 10

A Way Forward

Surrendering my clergy credentials was not part of a coordinated strategy for changes in church law and practice, except in the sense that it was a protest against what I considered to be "bad church law, applied legalistically and hurtfully." There was no overall design. Nor is a specific approach to revising church policy the basic theme of this book. Nevertheless, in this concluding chapter I want to discuss some possibilities. In addition to my work as a Christian ethicist I have played a fairly substantial role in church policy formation. As a delegate to four General Conferences, a member of two general church agencies, and a member of two general church task forces, I've had ample opportunity to see how things work and to take due note of possibilities and limitations.

Currently, The United Methodist Church is highly polarized around the issues discussed in this book. The most recent General Conference in 2016 was stymied in efforts to bridge the divides and to overcome serious conflicts. I was not a delegate to this conference, but I'm told that it was deeply frustrating to many who were. A decision was reached to avoid further legislation on the divisive sexuality issues and to create a special commission on the "way forward." This commission is to come up with plans to heal the divisions, to be presented to a specially called General Conference that would deal only with those issues in 2019—a year prior to the next regularly scheduled conference. The Commission on a Way Forward has been at work and is expected to provide a report to the Council of Bishops, possibly prior to publication of this book.

I am guardedly hopeful that this will prove successful, bearing in mind that the commission's recommendations will still have to be adopted by the much larger special General Conference. What I have to say in this chapter may prove useless, but I do want to add these thoughts to those of the preceding chapters.

What about GC 2019, Jan. 3rd Proposal

The Divided Church

The heart of the problem is deep division within The United Methodist Church (and to some extent other denominations) over the issues we have been exploring in this book. Divisions often appear within a local church; the problem the church faces is largely along regional and national lines. Support for changes in church teaching and law is largely—though not exclusively—located in the Northeast, North Central, and Western Jurisdictions. Opposition to change is largely located in the Southeast and South Central Jurisdictions. Opposition is even more pronounced in Africa, where UM conferences are growing most rapidly. Some who favor or oppose change are deeply committed. That is especially true of African United Methodists. The divisions will not be overcome easily. It appears, therefore, that the way forward will have to be marked by compromise.

Compromise on Church Teaching

As we have seen, the most divisive church teaching is contained in the words of one of the Social Principles holding that the practice of homosexuality is "incompatible with Christian teaching." The conclusion is simply stated, without explanation. Serious teaching on such a controversial statement requires more rationale. Exactly *why* is this incompatible with Christian teaching? Predictably the explanation would refer either to specific scriptural passages or to some version of natural law or to some blending of the two. The divisive conclusion cannot simply be stated if we are to have serious dialogue, looking toward a healing of divisions. I would, as I have said, have strong reservations about using a proof-texting rationale from Scripture. Those who disagree with me might not. So our conversation would center on biblical authority and how we relate our theology and ethics to the Bible. Similarly, if a natural law rationale is invoked, objections to that must be expressed forthrightly.

At the end of the day, there may still be divisions on these points; I expect there will be. That suggests to me that overcoming our divisions on church teaching means we accept the good faith of those who differ. We are not yet in a position to flatly express views that are opposed by a substantial number of fellow Methodists. The "state of the question" just isn't that clear yet.

Concretely, this means either the outright removal of the "incompatible with Christian teaching" section or some acknowledgment of different views. I favor the outright removal of that language. But if, as a compromise, some acknowledgment of differences needs to be stated, the provision could be reworded like this: "The question of homosexual practice has proved troublesome for the church. We acknowledge that people can, in good faith, have different views. Some believe it is incompatible with Christian teaching, while others consider it compatible with the gospel if it is an expression of morally disciplined, committed love." Such a formulation could at least be honest about where we are as a church. I do prefer simple deletion of the controverted words, but the other approach is a statement of the true situation and conveys a degree of mutual respect.

Two Points about Church Law

Church law is another matter. Two points should be borne in mind.

First is the view expressed by Thomas Aquinas that a ruler should avoid issuing laws that cannot be enforced. Aquinas was speaking of secular law in an era when law was generally issued by a single monarch or other ruler—that is, not democratically arrived at. So far as church law is concerned, I'm not aware that he applied the same principle. I believe it to be equally applicable. The problem, as stated by Aquinas, is that if a ruler establishes an unenforceable law, it leads to disrespect for all law. Unenforceable laws diminish respect for the lawgiver as well. That is why even good law should be enacted with restraint, particularly when it runs contrary to the conscience of many people. It may be better to wait until public opinion is more uniform and the law can be enforced without undue disruption.

The other point is similar: Too many laws, even if they are generally good ones, enervate the spirit of a populace. People become more driven by law than by values that are freely pursued. Too much regulation is a characteristic Methodist temptation, dating back to Wesley himself. Despite his very strong emphasis on love and grace, Wesley sought a high degree of discipline in organizations he led. That, essentially, is the origin of the name *Method*ist as applied to small groups he led. These were people who emphasized well-regulated *method*. To a point this was useful. But too much regulation can be a problem.

The heart of the problem with too much regulation is that people come to believe in and act out of the regulations more than the inner leading of the spirit and conscience. When Paul emphasized the priority of grace over law he was responding, in part, to a religious culture that had a huge number of laws, governing all sorts of things. Obedience to these laws, every one of them, was the essence of the spiritual life. Paul understood, to the contrary, that the essence of spiritual life is love, especially our loving response to God's free gift of grace. Translated into the "way forward" for the church, this means that we don't have to create a law or regulation for everything.

That is not to dismiss the importance of law out of hand. There need to be regulations. There needs to be a fabric of law, reflecting moral insight and institutional necessity. Much law is simply practical. Too little regulation isn't good for institutional life. Our quest is for the golden mean, defined by Aristotle as the zone "between excess and deficiency." The place of the golden mean will be subject to constant debate. But the fact remains that there can be too much law, even good law.

The Way Forward in Church Law

At this critical point in church history there has to be some compromise in our framing of church law. Some practical issues may not matter much. But what about legislation defining clergy eligibility and action?

On the question whether gay or lesbian persons could be ordained and appointed, we must remember that under our system there are many safeguards against approving (heterosexual) people for ministry who really shouldn't be ordained.

As chapter 4 makes clear, both ordained and lay members participate in that decision making. Why not simply trust that process? Someone like T. C. Morrow, eminently qualified for ministry, could be accepted for ordination, while those who are unqualified could be turned down. Does the church need to create absolute barriers such as the barriers that T. C. Morrow has faced?

In a conference in which most are opposed to ordaining somebody in a same-gender marriage, there isn't any current church law that would require the decision makers to approve them. I would regret the decision of any church body that was too prompted by prejudice, but in the absence of law nothing requires the acceptance of people who I might enthusiastically support. In time, the ability of a board of ordained ministry or a conference to block otherwise qualified people might be limited, but we're not there yet. Instead, we've gone much too far in the other direction of preventing a board or conference from accepting people whom they consider to be eminently qualified.

What, then, about clergy officiating at same-gender weddings? I was a delegate to the 1996 General Conference when that restriction was adopted. It was a surprise move and one that many of us greatly regretted. In a number of conferences, the actual effect has been clergy going ahead with that pastoral responsibility, in disregard of the prohibition. There have been some church trials as a result. More often, bishops and other church leaders have simply accepted the reality. One reason is that church trials are expensive, usually costing the church more than $80,000 — an amount often more than one conference staff member's annual salary and benefits. That seems a pretty steep price to pay for maintaining a prohibition that even the U.S. Supreme Court has ruled unconstitutional. Couldn't those who are opposed to change at least acknowledge that same-gender marriage is greatly preferable to promiscuity — and preferable even to psychologically frustrating enforced celibacy? I can't speak for those opposed to change in that church law, but we might think more seriously together about the actual alternatives.

Dealing with Regional and National Differences

The conflicts, in part, fall along regional and national fault lines. How are we to respond to areas of the church that are solidly committed to their positions? Think of the typical different stances between, say, much of Africa and much of the Western Jurisdiction. Is there a way forward that can encompass regional differences?

That may prove exceedingly difficult. There are those on both the left and the right who have openly advocated a split in the church. A prominent illustration comes from the UM Confessing Movement, which wrote this in response to the Commission on a Way Forward:

> The Commission must free itself of thinking of unity in terms of the denomination if it is to accomplish its purpose to "move us beyond the impasse over the nature, conditions, and extent of the inclusion of LGBTQ people within the church." Some sort of separation in which one part of the division would guarantee LGBTQ people ordination and same-sex marriage is required.
>
> We recognize that LGBTQ persons are as conscience bound in their demanding ordination and same sex marriage as we are in opposition. . . .
>
> If we affirm Scripture and tradition on the issues that divide us, we may live in communion but not under common governance.

Perhaps the disputes are so deep that it will ultimately come to a split, as it almost has in the worldwide Anglican community. I am not in favor of such schism, at least not now. We all have so much in common, historically, organizationally, and theologically. So much of our mission, including the funding of less prosperous parts of the church, is generally accepted by the denomination. Splits in American Methodism have endured for years, ultimately overcome with reunion. But if we can avoid such division we should.

If the tangled issues of church teaching and law cannot be resolved creatively, this may be the time to create greater regional autonomy. Perhaps, as some have suggested, American Methodism could become a distinct "central conference" in the pattern now operative in Africa, Europe, and the Philippines. (United Methodist conferences outside the United States are all governed by central conferences which, while also under the General Conference, have a good deal of autonomy.) Perhaps, in view of regional differences within the United States, the five regional jurisdictions could each become a separate central conference. If that were to develop, greater regional decision-making autonomy would have to be respected.

A further thought: If such regional and national division could be creatively devised, perhaps all parts of United Methodism might make more of the World Methodist Conference, a body that includes other churches with Wesleyan roots. I could envisage a number of the present boards and agencies of The United Methodist Church being restructured with that broader base.

Many within the church have concluded that we cannot simply limp along as we have been doing, with General Conferences increasingly manifesting animosity more than spiritual unity. I hope that, if it registers at all, my action in 2017 will contribute to the healing process.

Epilogue

*E*vents have moved along during the year following my surrender of ordination at the 2017 Baltimore Washington Conference. In May 2018, the United Methodist Council of Bishops adopted a proposal to the 2019 special session of the General Conference calling for the removal of restrictive language from the *Book of Discipline*, which would enable regional bodies and local churches to allow pastors to perform same-gender marriages and to authorize the ordination of gay and lesbian persons of good qualifications and character to be ordained.

A very unexpected thing happened in respect to my own ordination. When I surrendered my credentials, as reported in this book, I understood this to be irrevocable and final. At the time I did not fully understand what this meant legally. When I handed over my ordination papers to the bishop in 2017, I thought that was it, over and done with. But there is a provision that I didn't know about: that the clergy executive session of the conference would have to vote on whether or not to accept my action. In my absence, almost exactly one year later, the clergy voted, by a strong majority, not to accept my surrendered ordination. Legally this meant that I was still an ordained United Methodist minister. Being ushered back into the closed session I was deeply moved by a warm standing ovation of some four hundred clergy colleagues. I would like to believe, and do believe, that they were signaling agreement with my views and actions on bad church law, applied legalistically and hurtfully. In thanking them, I reiterated my feelings about the issues at hand.

That was prior to any action on the commissioning of T. C. Marrow. I had been pleased that the conference board of ordained ministry decided to present her to the conference for commissioning. But to my deep disappointment the board and bishop reversed that action. She would not be presented because of the extremely narrow Judicial Council ruling that being in a same-gender marriage precluded acceptance into ordained ministry. The clergy session would not be permitted to vote on Marrow. The bishop's ruling was formally appealed by a large majority vote of the assembled clergy. It will be up to the Judicial Council to decide. Given the conservative cast of that council, I am not optimistic about the outcome. Still, the actions by the upcoming special General Conference session can make that unimportant. And I do appreciate our bishop's support of what the Council of Bishops is advocating.

Meanwhile, I confronted a dilemma: Should I repeat that action of a year ago, again surrendering my credentials? I struggled with that. But in face of clear evidence that a strong majority of clergy colleagues were also seeking change, I concluded that my point had already been made. I should work with them from inside the circle, at least for now, where I can seek with others to represent those who had been excluded.

Earlier in this book I referred to "sin" as attitudes, actions, and practices that create barriers to receiving the free, unqualified gift of God's grace. At an individual level we often create such sinful barriers and we seek healing and restoration. But we also sin at a corporate, institutional level, with attitudes and actions that create barriers to receiving the free and unqualified gift of God's grace. The events of this year have given me greater energy and insight into the task of confronting and healing the sin of the church.

The deeper theological, ethical, and pastoral issues addressed in this book will continue to be part of the church's ongoing conversation not only within The United Methodist Church but also in other Christian denominations. I believe the results will be positive, both in respect to the sexuality-related issues and in wider issues as Christians seek deeper grounding in the faith and greater relevance in a troubled world. God is incomprehensibly greater than any of us, and we are all embraced in the grace that binds us to God and to one another.

Notes

CHAPTER 1: THEOLOGICAL MEANING OF ORDINATION

"A United Methodist statement" The United Methodist statement on ordination is from *The Book of Discipline of the United Methodist Church 2016* (Nashville: United Methodist Publishing House, 2016), par. 303. The Disciples of Christ document on ministry quoted here is Theological Foundations and Policies and Criteria for the Ordering of Ministry of the Christian Church (Disciples of Christ), 2009, available on the church's website at disciples.org/wp-content/uploads/2014/07/TFPCOM-Final.pdf.

"two trillion galaxies" There remains uncertainty about the total number of galaxies and the average number of stars in galaxies. With the help of the Hubble telescope, NASA is revising previous ideas. The estimate of two trillion galaxies is from NASA, "Hubble Reveals Observable Universe Contains 10 Times More Galaxies Than Previously Thought," October 13, 2016, https://www.nasa.gov/feature/goddard/2016/hubble -reveals-observable-universe-contains-10-times-more-galaxies-than -previously-thought; and Marina Koren, "The Universe Just Got 10 Times More Interesting," *Atlantic*, October 14, 2016, https://www.theatlantic .com/science/archive/2016/10/so-many-galaxies/504185/. Elizabeth Howell reports that current research is concluding that the Milky Way contains around 100 billion stars; see "How Many Stars Are in the Universe?" Space.com, May 17, 2017, https://www.space.com/26078-how-many -stars-are-there.html; and "How Many Stars Are in the Milky Way?" Space.com, March 29, 2018, https://www.space.com/25959-how-many -stars-are-in-the-milky-way.html Such estimates vary among cosmologists, but all agree that the total number of stars is vast beyond

comprehension. Indeed, the claim that there are more stars in the universe than grains of sand on all the beaches of the world is now broadly accepted.

"Creation is the external—and only the external—basis of the covenant" The Barth quotation is from *Church Dogmatics*, III/1, *The Doctrine of Creation* (Edinburgh: T. and T. Clark, 1958), 97.

CHAPTER 3: PASTORAL MEANING OF ORDINATION

"The joys and the hopes" The encyclical *Gaudium et Spes* (Pastoral Constitution on the Church in the Modern World), promulgated by Pope Paul VI on December 7, 1965, is available on the Vatican's website at http://www.vatican.va/archive/hist_councils/ii_vatican_council/documents/vat-ii_const_19651207_gaudium-et-spes_en.html.

"John Wesley, founder of Methodism" The discussion of John Wesley as spiritual leader, and his dialogue with Bishop Butler, is from Richard M. Cameron, ed., *The Rise of Methodism: A Source Book* (New York: Philosophical Library, 1954), 282, 288–89.

CHAPTER 6: THE PAINFUL DECISION

"The practice of homosexuality is incompatible with Christian teaching" The statement on homosexuality being "incompatible with Christian teaching" is from *The Book of Discipline of the United Methodist Church 2016* (Nashville: United Methodist Publishing House, 2016), par. 304.3. In the Social Principles in the *Book of Discipline*, that phrase is in par. 161-G.

CHAPTER 7: THEOLOGICAL PERSPECTIVE

"Grace pervades our understanding of Christian faith and life" The statements on United Methodist doctrine are from *The Book of Discipline of the United Methodist Church 2016* (Nashville: United Methodist Publishing House, 2016), par. 102.

CHAPTER 8: ETHICAL IMPLICATIONS

"Clinicians should be aware" The statements on therapy by the American Academy of Child and Adolescent Psychiatry are from "Practice Parameter on Gay, Lesbian, or Bisexual Sexual Orientation, Gender Nonconformity, and Gender Discordance in Children and Adolescents," *Journal of the American Academy of Child and Adolescent Psychiatry* 51, no. 9 (September 2012): 957–74. The statement was updated in 2018; see http://www.hrc.org/blog/aacap-adopts-new-policy-statement-on-conversion-therapy.

"No union is more profound than marriage"   Justice Anthony Kennedy's statement in defense of same-gender marriage is from the conclusion of the majority opinion in Obergefell v. Hodges, 576 U. S. (2015). The complete U.S. Supreme Court decision is available on the court's website at https://www.supremecourt.gov/opinions/slipopinion/14.

"the word 'sex' . . . the word 'gender'"   Another important distinction between "sex" and "gender," which is beyond the point I am making about my use of "same-gender," is that "sex" is biological, or chromosomal; whereas "gender" is fluid and relates to social roles and a person's self-identification as a man or woman or somewhere in between.

CHAPTER 10: A WAY FORWARD

"The Commission must free itself"   The quotation from the UM Confessing Movement is from its written response to the Commission on a Way Forward, June 6, 2017.

CPSIA information can be obtained
at www.ICGtesting.com
Printed in the USA
FSHW01n0219160918
52186FS